GUANTÁNAMO KID
THE TRUE STORY OF MOHAMMED EL-GHARANI

First published in English in 2019
by SelfMadeHero
139–141 Pancras Road
London NW1 1UN
www.selfmadehero.com

English translation © 2019 SelfMadeHero

Written by Jérôme Tubiana and illustrated by Alexandre Franc
English text by Jérôme Tubiana and Edward Gauvin

Publishing Director: Emma Hayley
Sales & Marketing Manager: Sam Humphrey
Editorial & Production Manager: Guillaume Rater
Designers: Txabi Jones and Kate McLauchlan
UK Publicist: Paul Smith
With thanks to: Nick de Somogyi

First published in French by Dargaud in 2018
© Dargaud 2018, by El-Gorani, Franc & Tubiana
www.dargaud.com
All rights reserved

INSTITUT
FRANÇAIS
ROYAUME-UNI

This book is supported by the Institut français (Royaume-Uni) as
part of the Burgess programme

A CIP record for this book is available from the British Library

ISBN: 978-1-910593-66-0

10 9 8 7 6 5 4 3 2 1

Printed and bound in Slovenia

JÉRÔME TUBIANA • ALEXANDRE FRANC

GUANTÁNAMO KID
THE TRUE STORY OF MOHAMMED EL-GHARANI

SELF
MADE
HERO

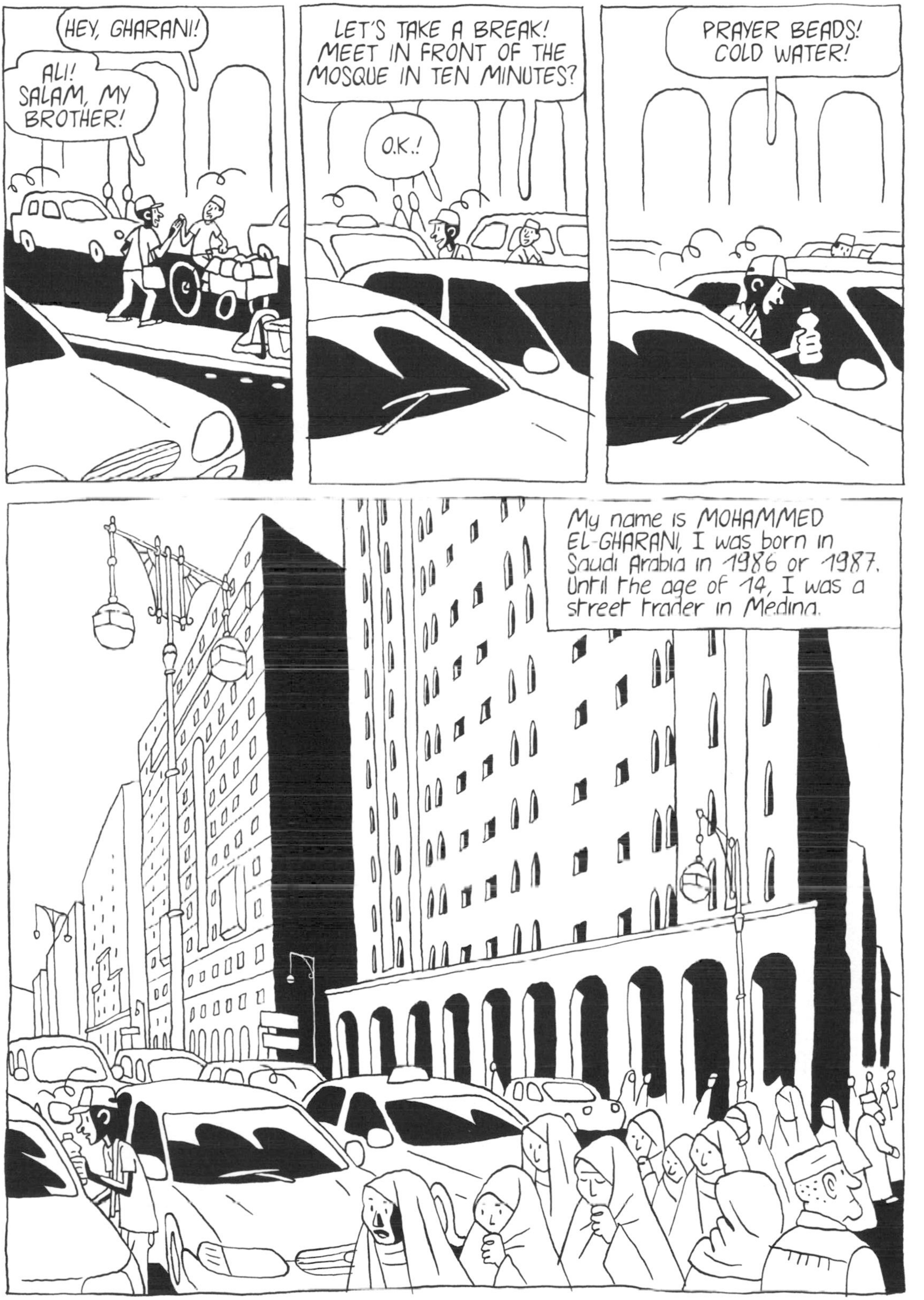
HEY, GHARANI!
ALI! SALAM, MY BROTHER!
LET'S TAKE A BREAK! MEET IN FRONT OF THE MOSQUE IN TEN MINUTES?
O.K.!
PRAYER BEADS! COLD WATER!
My name is MOHAMMED EL-GHARANI, I was born in Saudi Arabia in 1986 or 1987. Until the age of 14, I was a street trader in Medina.

My family came from North Chad, I don't know exactly where. I do know that it's the desert there — my grandparents were nomads, from the Goran tribe. When they arrived in Medina, they took the tribe's name as our surname — Gharani. When I was a kid, I didn't know anything about this, our tribe, our country. My father only told us that, starting when he was seven, he wandered alone for days in the desert to find grass for the camels.

My grandparents had moved to Medina because they wanted to pray in the mosque of the Prophet. We believe that if you live in Medina, it's easier to get to Paradise.

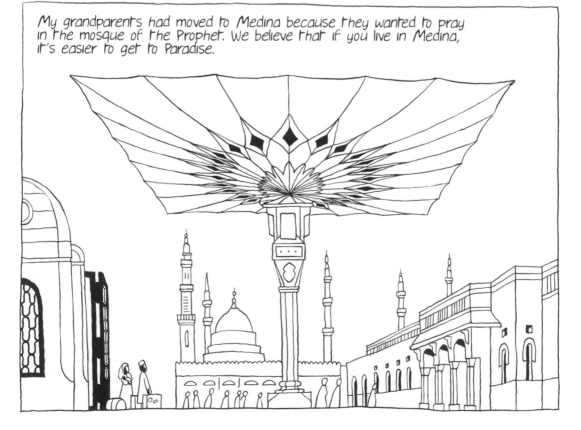

Paradise: after an Islamic miniature.

When they arrived in Saudi Arabia, my father did a lot of different jobs: washing cars, working in a shop belonging to a Saudi... Because you can't own a shop if you're not Saudi.

There are a lot of stupid rules about foreigners in Saudi Arabia. For example, when my parents tried to send me to school:

IS HE SAUDI?

NO, CHADIAN.

THERE ARE NO PLACES LEFT, BUT COME BACK NEXT MONTH...

WELCOME

So when I was eight, I went to a private school run by a Chadian. In his house, he taught kids from Chad, Sudan, Egypt, Pakistan... I was there for four years. After two years, my father became ill.

Then my elder brother and I had to work. We sold stuff in the street.

PRAYER-BEADS! COLD WATER!

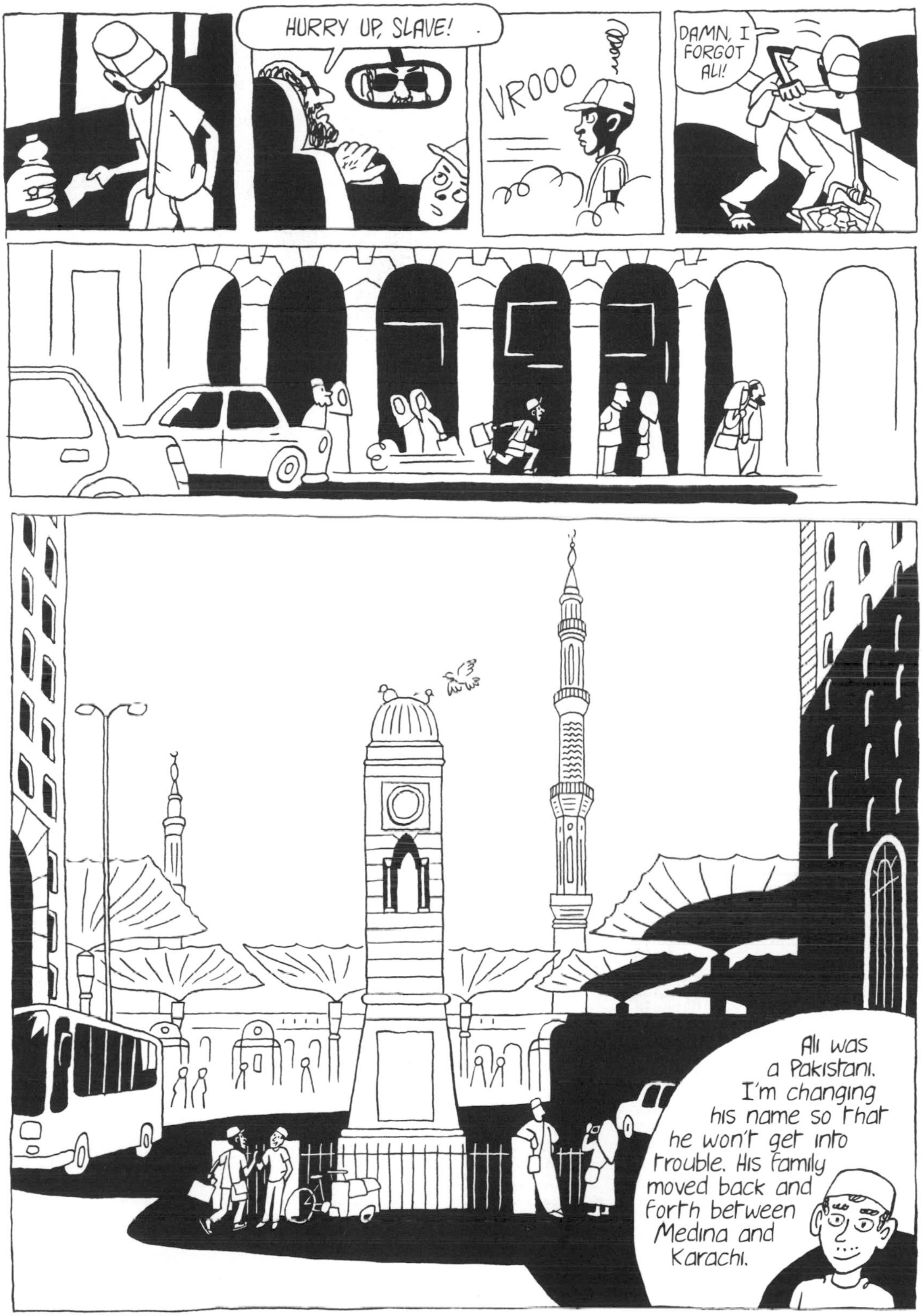
HURRY UP, SLAVE!
VROOO
DAMN, I FORGOT ALI!
Ali was a Pakistani. I'm changing his name so that he won't get into trouble. His family moved back and forth between Medina and Karachi.

With Ali and other kids, I went to Mecca from time to time to sell stuff to pilgrims. You can make good money during the Hajj and Ramadan.

PRAYER-BEADS! PRAYER-MATS! COLD WATER!

All day long we stood at the crossroads and when the bus stopped, we had a few seconds to sell our stuff. We worked up to fourteen hours a day. We had to be careful...

THE POLICE!

If they caught you, they'd take your money and confiscate your stuff. Sometimes they'd take you to prison and your father had to come and sign a piece of paper so that you could be released.

Living this life, you become tough.

Ali taught me some Urdu, his mother tongue: numbers, words you need for selling, anything that's useful with the Pakistani pilgrims.

ONE?

AYK!

TWO?

DEO!

YOU'RE GOOD AT LANGUAGES! IF YOU COULD SPEAK ENGLISH, YOU COULD WORK IN A HOTEL IN MECCA... MY BROTHER SPEAKS ENGLISH, HE'S GOT A GOOD JOB AS A HOTEL RECEPTIONIST.

I'D LIKE TO BECOME A DENTIST...

DENTIST! ALRIGHT! YOU'LL FILL OUR CAVITIES FOR US!...

YEAH!

'CAUSE HERE, FOR A FOREIGNER TO FIND A GOOD DENTIST...

GOOD DENTISTS ARE ONLY FOR THE SAUDIS.

BUT IT'S NO USE DREAMING...

NO.

TO BECOME A DENTIST, YOU'LL HAVE TO STUDY.

YEAH...

...AND UNIVERSITY IS ONLY FOR THE SAUDIS!

BUT HOW LONG ARE YOU GONNA WORK IN THE STREET? ALL YOUR LIFE?

NO.

YESTERDAY, IN THE SOUK, I SPOKE WITH OMAR. YOU KNOW, THE ONE WHO SELLS COMPUTERS...

WHEN A COMPUTER IS BROKEN, I HAVE TO SEND IT TO JEDDAH. HERE, NO ONE KNOWS HOW TO FIX THEM. YOU KNOW ANYTHING ABOUT COMPUTERS, HMM?

I HAVE AN UNCLE WHO TEACHES COMPUTERS IN KARACHI...

I WON'T GO TO PAKISTAN...

WHY NOT? MY UNCLES AND COUSINS WILL WELCOME YOU, YOU JUST NEED TO PAY FOR THE LESSONS. THEN, WHEN YOU'RE BACK, YOU COULD BORROW SOME MONEY AND SET UP A COMPUTER REPAIR WORKSHOP!

NOW YOU'RE DREAMING...

NO, YOU CAN DO IT!

THINK ABOUT IT. THE RAIN STARTS WITH A DROP OF WATER...

I HAVE TO GO BACK TO WORK...

BUT I'LL REMEMBER THIS NICE DREAM BEFORE I GO TO BED TONIGHT... BYE!

Over the next few days, I kept thinking over what we'd said.

PAKISTAN?...

I was used to traveling inside Saudi Arabia by myself. I started to travel alone when I was 10 and never stopped. Even though my elder brother often beat me when I returned...

My father allowed me to go to Mecca, Jeddah or Riyadh, but he refused to let me leave the country.

On the other hand, Ali was right: could I work in the street all my life?...

14

Since starting to work, I'd saved up some money. So I decided to go.

JEDDAH
جدة

WHERE HAVE YOU BEEN FOR THE PAST TWO DAYS?! WE LOOKED FOR YOU EVERYWHERE, WE WERE WORRIED SICK!...

I WANT TO GO TO PAKISTAN TO STUDY ENGLISH AND I.T.

WHAT'S MY FUTURE HERE? LIFE HERE IS MORE AND MORE EXPENSIVE... LET ME GO TO STUDY. I'LL MAKE MONEY AND IT WILL BENEFIT THE WHOLE FAMILY.

BUT WHY PAKISTAN? YOU'RE CRAZY, MY NEPHEW!...

YOU'RE STILL A CHILD, MOHAMMED. YOUR PLACE IS WITH YOUR PARENTS.

THINK OF YOUR MOTHER. YOU DON'T WANT TO UPSET HER, DO YOU?

At the Chadian consulate in Jeddah.

I'VE COME HERE BEFORE. THIS TIME, I HAVE EVERYTHING.

ARE YOU CHADIAN?

YES.

YOU GOT NO PASSPORT?

NO.

HOW OLD ARE YOU?

FOURTEEN... OR THIRTEEN, I'M NOT SURE.

AT YOUR AGE, YOU'RE NOT ALLOWED TO TRAVEL ALONE. YOU NEED TO LIE ABOUT YOUR AGE. WE'LL SAY YOU'RE 18. AND YOU NEED TO CHANGE YOUR NAME. WHAT'S YOUR NAME?

(MOHAMMED HAMID ALI.)

NOW YOU'LL BE YOUSEF. ALRIGHT?

NO PROBLEM.

YOUSEF... ABAKIR... SALEH. GOOD?

ALRIGHT.

YOU HAVE MONEY?

YES.

I had to give him 500 riyals instead of 200, but I got my passport.

Then I went to the Pakistani consulate and I got my visa.

Now I was called Yousef Abakir Saleh. That fake name was the beginning of my problems with the Americans...

But back then, I had no idea.

V. **Allegations Regarding FBI Participation in Interrogation of Detainee Yousef Abkir Salih Al Qarani**

In this Section we address the conduct of FBI agents, together with the military, in the interrogation of detainee Yousef Abkir Saleh Al Qarani (#269) at GTMO. We determined that in September 2003, FBI agents

I WILL STAY WITH ALI'S COUSINS. I'LL BE GONE SIX MONTHS FOR THE LESSONS AND THEN I'LL COME BACK. IT'LL ALL BE O.K.

IF IT'S REALLY WHAT YOU WANT, MY SON, YOU CAN GO. LET'S COLLECT SOME MONEY FROM THE FAMILY TO PAY FOR YOUR TRIP...

BUT...

DON'T WORRY... HOW COULD HE LEAVE? HE'S GOT NO PASSPORT, OR ANY MONEY...

HE'S SO YOUNG... IT CAN WAIT A BIT...

GOOD NIGHT...

Uncle ABDERRAHMAN is my mother's younger brother. On my last day in Medina, I went to see him.

MY FAVORITE NEPHEW! STRANGE HOUR TO VISIT!...

FORGIVE ME, UNCLE ABDERRAHMAN...

I couldn't say it out loud, but in my heart I knew it was goodbye. I think he understood.

MY SISTER, YOUR SON MUST HAVE LEFT.

MAYBE HE JUST WENT TO JEDDAH, LIKE HE USUALLY DOES...

NO. HE'S GONE MUCH FURTHER AWAY THIS TIME.

19

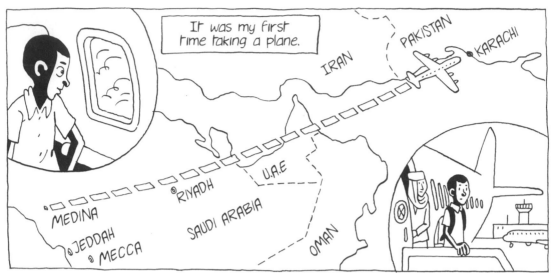

I landed in Karachi and called my parents from there. They were angry! Even Ali was surprised that I had managed to get there. His uncle and his cousin picked me up at the airport and brought me to their house. They reassured my parents on the phone.

BECAUSE YOU'RE FROM MEDINA, I'LL GIVE YOU A GOOD PRICE. AND YOU CAN LIVE HERE WITH US FOR FREE.

Everybody was so nice to me. And because I'm from Medina, people came out of their houses to shake hands with me.

Ali's uncle was a teacher, in charge of the 30-odd kids he taught from home. Most were Pakistani, but there were also some foreigners. Only me and the family's children lived in the house, though. I didn't feel like a stranger. I was at home.

The lessons were to last six months, three months of English lessons, then another three of English and I.T., at the end of which I planned to go home.

Every Friday, my family called. My mum called every two or three days.

Two months after I got there, 9/11 happened. I didn't really pay much attention...

I was playing football with the neighborhood kids. In Medina, people fought to get me on their team! I was a fan of HAMZA SALEH, a Goran from Medina who had been chosen twice for the Saudi national team, once in 1994 and once in 1998. All the Goran kids dreamt of playing like him so that they could get Saudi citizenship.

Every day, I woke up, went to school, ate lunch, played football, studied, prayed. I was very busy with my lessons.

Every Friday, I went to pray in a big mosque not far from the house. Most of the people there were Arabs, because the imam was Saudi and spoke good Arabic.

HEY YOU!

SAUDI?

NO, CHADIAN.

DON'T LIE, YOU'RE SAUDI!

I think they recognized my accent.

They took me to a prison where they started questioning me.

LISTEN, AMERICANS ARE GOING TO INTERROGATE YOU. JUST SAY YOU'RE FROM AL-QAIDA, AND THEY'LL SEND YOU HOME WITH SOME MONEY.

WHAT ARE YOU TALKING ABOUT?

TELL THE AMERICANS YOU WENT WITH AL-QAIDA TO AFGHANISTAN, O.K.?!...

WHY WOULD I LIE?

Al-Qaida: I had never heard that word before.

They hung me by my arms and beat me.

WHERE IS OSAMA BIN LADEN?

WHO'S THAT?...

STOP FUCKING WITH US! YOU'RE AL-QAIDA, YES!

A Pakistani was in the room, behind the Americans. When they asked if I was from al-Qaida, he nodded, to tell me to say yes.

Some tortured me with electricity, others just signed a piece of paper claiming they had done so.

We have a Goran saying: "Awondra turu za shi." People are like the fingers of a hand: they're not all the same.

I started to recognize the Pakistani guards...

If I saw who was coming, I knew if there would be torture or not.

One Pakistani officer was a good guy. He gave us food and water, and he even helped some of us to escape.

I CAN'T RELEASE ALL OF YOU, ONLY SOME OF YOU...

He brought the guards hashish, and while they smoked outside, he talked with us. Once he said:

THE PAKISTANI GOVERNMENT WANTS TO SELL YOU TO THE AMERICANS, 5,000 DOLLARS EACH.

"First Poem of My Life"

MOVE IT CAUTIOUSLY IN THE LAND OF THOSE WHO SPEAK NO ARABIC*!

*PAKISTAN

EVEN IF THEY GAVE YOU OATHS BOUND BY OATHS, THEIR AIM IS TO WORSHIP PETTY CASH AND FOR IT THEY BREAK ALL VOWS. I CAME TO THEIR LAND TO PURSUE AN EDUCATION, AND SAW SUCH MALICE AMONG THEM. THEY SURROUNDED THE MOSQUE, WEAPONS DRAWN, AS IF THEY WERE IN A FIELD OF WAR.

They said to us:

COME OUT PEACEFULLY, AND DON'T UTTER A SINGLE WORD.

INTO A TRANSPORT TRUCK THEY LIFTED US, AND IN SHACKLES OF INJUSTICE THEY BOUND US. FOR SIXTEEN HOURS WE WALKED; FOR THE ENTIRE TIME WE REMAINED IN SHACKLES. ALL OF US WANTED TO EVACUATE OUR BOWELS BUT THEY INSISTED ON DENYING US.

THE SOLDIER STRUCK WITH HIS BOOT; HE SAID WE WERE ALL EQUALLY SUBJECTS. IN THE PRISON'S DARKNESS THEY SPREAD US OUT, IN THE COLD'S BITTERNESS WE SAT.

Mohammed El-Gharani

27

When they heard we were going to be sold to the Americans, some panicked.

But I was kind of happy.

All I knew of the Americans was what I saw on T.V.

I loved watching old cowboy movies...

I believed what I had seen in the films, that Americans were good people. I would have the right to a lawyer...

Maybe they would even let me study in the U.S. before sending me back to my parents.

They started taking detainees away every night, in groups of 20. We didn't know where they were going, but we thought they were being moved to the U.S. One night, it was my group's turn.

They made us change into blue overalls. At first, they had chained us together by our feet and wrists. Now they replaced the chains with shackles and handcuffs.

But I was happy. I thought the Americans would figure out the truth, that they would realize the Pakistanis had tricked them, and they would send me back to Saudi Arabia.

I really could not have imagined how Americans were going to treat me.

LOOK, WE'RE GOING TO THE U.S.!

DON'T SAY THAT!

SHUT UP!

Later, in Guantánamo, I never stopped wondering why I had been arrested. I discussed this with my friends.

YOU WERE IN THE WRONG PLACE AT THE WRONG TIME...

So my hands were shackled behind my back and a guard was holding me by a chain. There were 20 of us, with maybe 15 guards. They covered our eyes and ears with masks and put us in a truck. When they took off our masks, we were at an airport. Then the movie started.

YOU'RE UNDER ARREST!

YOU'RE IN THE CUSTODY OF THE U.S. ARMY!

U.S. ARMY

DON'T TALK, DON'T MOVE, OR WE'LL SHOOT YOU!

An interpreter translated into Arabic.

They started beating us.

People were bleeding and crying. It lasted maybe half an hour.

We were almost unconscious when they put us in a helicopter. They didn't tell us where we were going.

In the helicopter, I was mad at the Americans and I started to hate them.

HOPEFULLY THOSE ATTACKS AGAINST AMERICA WILL HAPPEN AGAIN! IT MUST HAVE BEEN A PUNISHMENT FROM GOD.

Later, in Guantánamo, I understood that even if many Americans are bad people and care only about themselves, there are still a lot of good people among them. "Awondra turu za shi."

We landed at another airstrip.

YOU'RE TERRORISTS, CRIMINALS, WE'RE GOING TO KILL YOU!

It was the first time I heard the N-word...

YOU, FUCKING NIGGER!

There was racism in Saudi Arabia, but in Guantánamo I learned that there are truly racist people.

FUCKING NIGGER!

I asked a British-Pakistani prisoner what that meant.

YOU DON'T WANNA KNOW. IT'S A BAD WORD.

I asked another brother from Saudi Arabia.

SOMEBODY CALLED YOU A NIGGER? THEY CALLED YOU THAT?

FUCKING NIGGER!

WASSUP, HONKY? WHITE TRASH!

The guard who insulted me was young, between 20 and 25, like most of the guards. He was an idiot. I waited for a chance.

HEY MAN, LONG TIME NO SEE!...

YOU'RE NOT ANGRY ANYMORE?

NAH.

FUCK, HE BROKE MY TOOTH!

YOU SEE THAT?

They sprayed me with pepper spray, something they used often. It burnt and it made it very hard to breathe.

He wasn't the only guard I hit in the face. And I even pissed in others' faces. I was a bad boy in Guantánamo.

32

After I was taken out from the helicopter, just after I heard "nigger" for the first time, they beat me up again. Then they took off my clothes and put me inside a tent.

A man wearing a U.S. uniform spoke to me in Arabic. He was an Egyptian, I recognized his dialect.

WHEN WAS THE LAST TIME YOU SAW OSAMA BIN LADEN?

WHO?

They beat me up again.

Throughout my time on this base, I was beaten.

HERE'S THE CAN!

I wondered where I was. It was very cold and it was impossible to sleep.

As soon as we went to sleep, at 10 p.m., the soldiers started shouting.

GET UP! GET UP!

Every three hours, they searched us.

GET UP! GET UP!

Or they threw buckets of cold water on us.

IT WILL WARM YOU UP!

IS THAT YOUR HOLY BOOK?

CAN'T YOU PUT IT WHERE IT BELONGS?!

Another interrogation:

WHY COVER YOURSELF? YOU ASHAMED?

EMBARRASSED? I'LL SNIP IT OFF FOR YA!

One day, they gave out clothes and moved us into tents.

RED CROSS MIGHT PAY YOU A VISIT SOON.

Another day:

WE CAUGHT THE TERRORISTS!

35

WE'VE BEEN FIGHTING THEM. THEY KILLED LOTS OF PEOPLE!

HERE ARE THEIR GUNS!

It wasn't the Red Cross.

Then they brought dogs and put them on our backs to scare us.

AFGHANISTAN

KANDAHAR

PAKISTAN

KARACHI

I spent a month at this American base. Later on, I found out it was in Kandahar, Afghanistan.

They started moving prisoners again, every night, in groups of twenty.

They'd take you from your tent, strip you naked, shave your head and beard (though I was too young to have a beard), then beat you up.

They'd stick you in an orange jumpsuit, handcuff you and chain your feet, and make you wear mittens so you couldn't get out of the handcuffs.

They'd also put dark goggles and big headphones on you, so you almost couldn't hear.

YOU BOYS ARE GOING SOMEWHERE THE SUN DON'T SHINE! THE MOON NEITHER! THERE AIN'T NO FREEDOM THERE. THAT'S WHERE YOU'RE SPENDING THE REST OF YOUR LIVES!

With all that on, you don't feel time passing. But I could hear the changing of the guard, probably every hour. I must have spent five hours sitting on a bench, back to back with another detainee. We weren't allowed to talk. Some of us were crying because of the pain, and they were struck across the face. Then we were put in a plane.

USAF

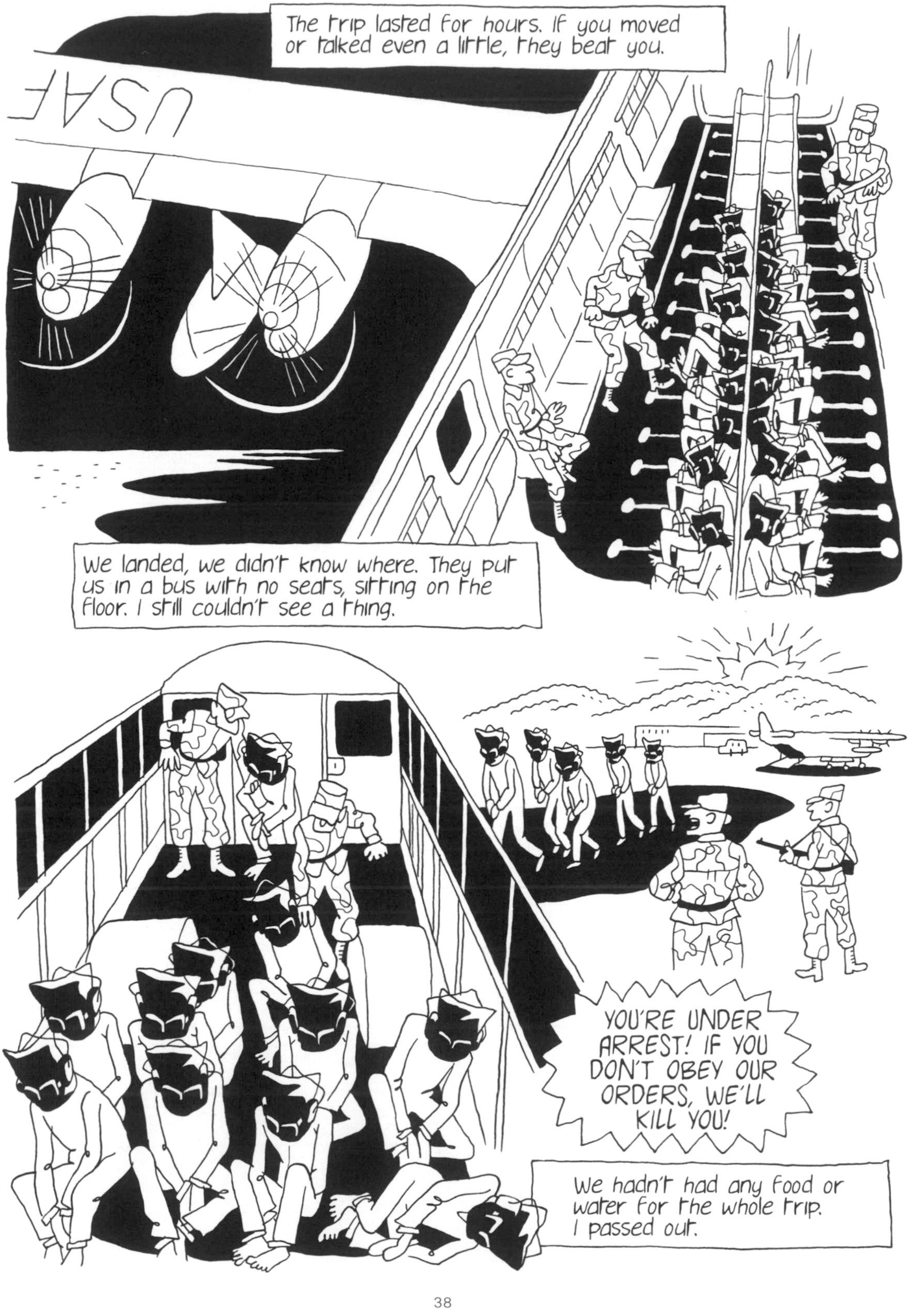
The trip lasted for hours. If you moved or talked even a little, they beat you.
USAF
We landed, we didn't know where. They put us in a bus with no seats, sitting on the floor. I still couldn't see a thing.
YOU'RE UNDER ARREST! IF YOU DON'T OBEY OUR ORDERS, WE'LL KILL YOU!
We hadn't had any food or water for the whole trip. I passed out.

I woke up hearing voices questioning me in different languages. My dark goggles were gone. I saw medics around me, and I had an I.V. in my arm.

They took me to a cell. I saw soldiers everywhere, and guns, like it was a war zone. There were high metal fences, too. My cell had no walls, no roof, no shelter from the sun or the rain. Just wire netting.

We were in Guantánamo, in Camp X-Ray.*

*The first prisoners from Afghanistan were held in Camp X-Ray from 21 January 2002. In April 2002, X-Ray was closed and the prisoners transferred to Delta, a permanent structure.

The night I arrived, when I was still exhausted from the flight, I was subjected to my first interrogation.

WE HAVE TWO FACES. ONE NICE, ONE UGLY.

WE DON'T WANT TO HAVE TO SHOW YOU THE UGLY ONE.

WHAT WERE YOU DOING IN AFGHANISTAN?

ARE YOU WITH AL-QAIDA?

NO.

ARE YOU TALIBAN?

NO.

WERE YOU IN A TRAINING CAMP?

NO, NO, NO!

IF YOU DON'T WANT TO COOPERATE, WE'LL GET THE TRUTH OUT OF YOU!

PUT HIM BACK IN HIS CELL!

I was tired and scared. Somewhere or other they were torturing prisoners. When you hear them screaming, you're really scared — you think you'll be next.

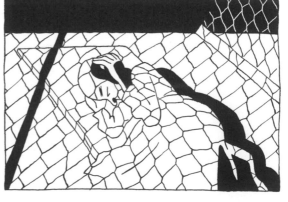

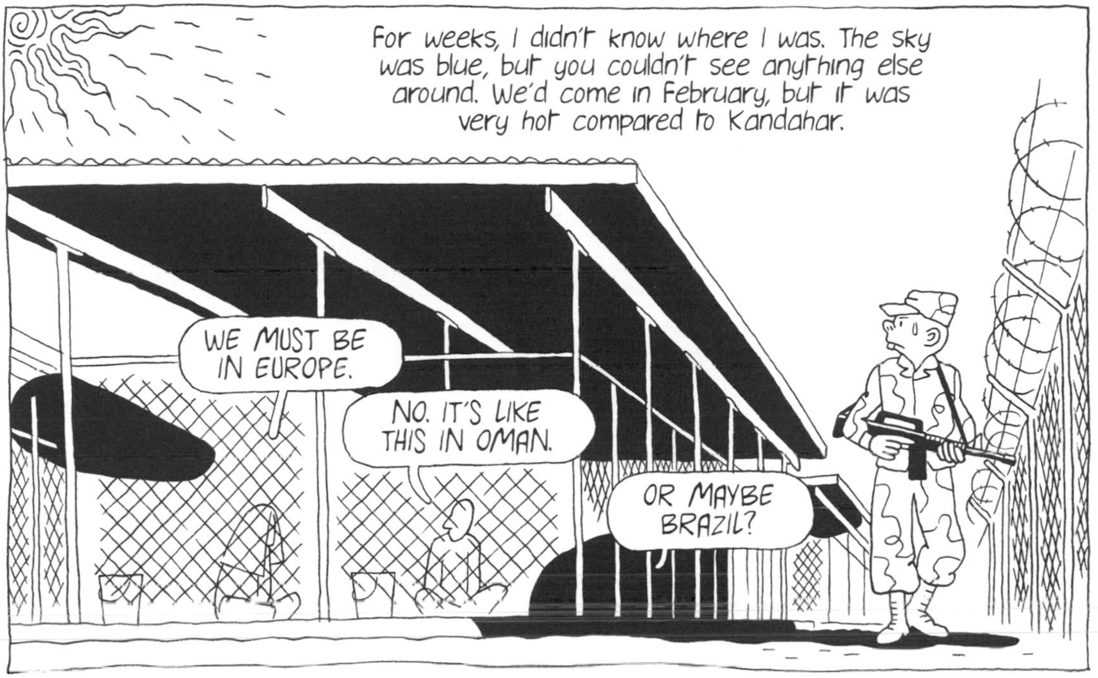
For weeks, I didn't know where I was. The sky was blue, but you couldn't see anything else around. We'd come in February, but it was very hot compared to Kandahar.
WE MUST BE IN EUROPE.
NO. IT'S LIKE THIS IN OMAN.
OR MAYBE BRAZIL?

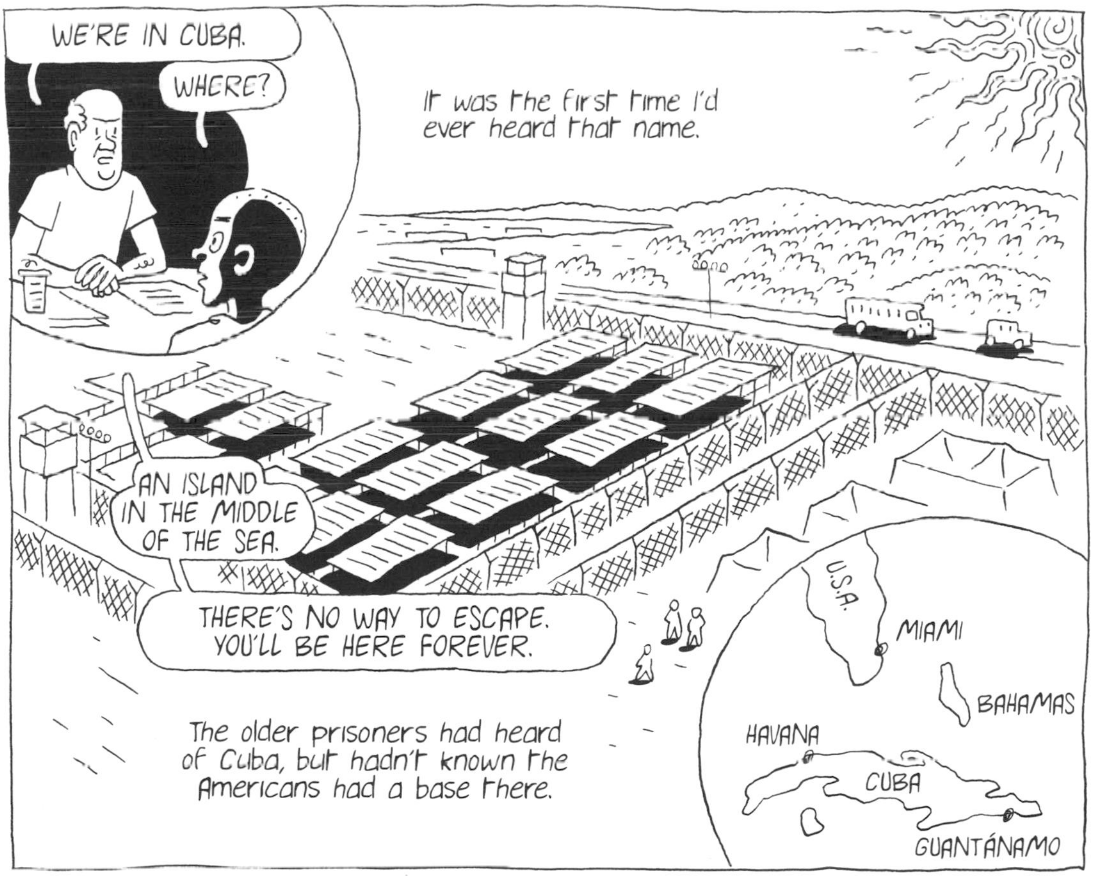
WE'RE IN CUBA.
WHERE?
It was the first time I'd ever heard that name.
AN ISLAND IN THE MIDDLE OF THE SEA.
THERE'S NO WAY TO ESCAPE. YOU'LL BE HERE FOREVER.
The older prisoners had heard of Cuba, but hadn't known the Americans had a base there.
U.S.A.
MIAMI
BAHAMAS
HAVANA
CUBA
GUANTÁNAMO

Guantánamo is like a war zone. Guards, guns, helicopters flying overhead, as if to show us we're really bad people. They want to make you feel like you're dangerous.

They searched us once a day, sometimes twice. Every time, they'd shackle our hands and feet, and give us a thorough going-over.

Sometimes they'd string you up like a chicken and hit you in the back. Sometimes they chained you up with your face on the ground. You couldn't move for 16 or 17 hours. You had to piss where you lay.

FEEL LIKE COOPERATING?

Sometimes they showed you their ugly face: just torture, torture without any questions.

WE'LL FUCK YOU!

!....

At first, there were interrogations every night. They tortured me with electricity, mostly on my toes. The nails of my big toes came off.

I HAVE A RIGHT TO AN ATTORNEY.

NOT HERE IN GUANTÁNAMO, YOU DON'T! YOU GOT NO RIGHTS HERE!

If you said yes, they stopped the torture. If you said no, they kept it going. It could go on all day. Sometimes, they'd even get tired of it themselves. Sometimes the interrogator would come in the morning, and if you didn't want to talk, he'd leave you to the guards and come back that night.

YOU'RE JUST A SLAVE! WE BOUGHT YOU FROM THE PAKISTANIS!

Sometimes I'd say:

YES!

I'LL SAY YES TO WHATEVER YOU WANT!

Because I just wanted the torture to stop. But the next day, I'd say: "No, I said yes yesterday because of the torture."

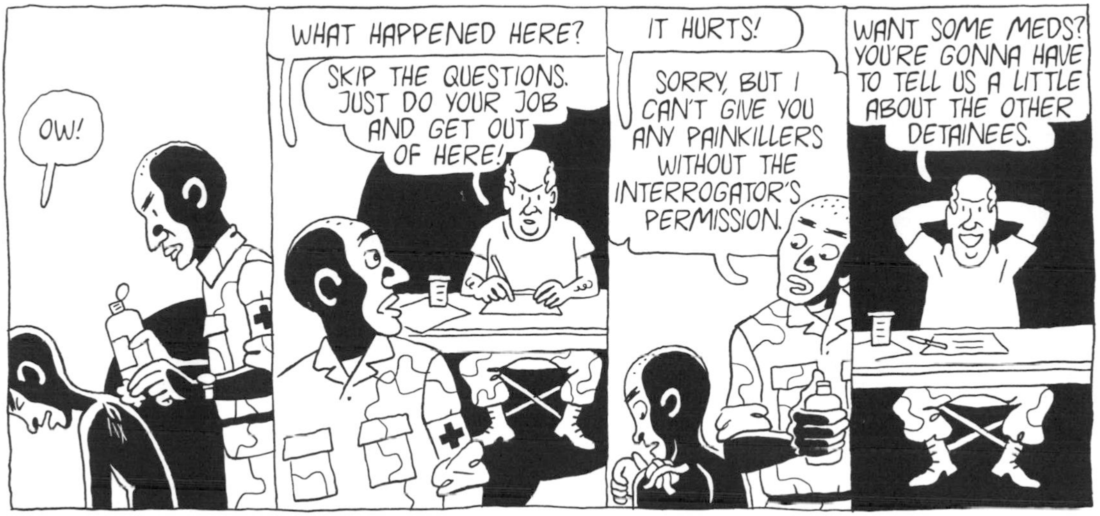
OW!
WHAT HAPPENED HERE?
SKIP THE QUESTIONS. JUST DO YOUR JOB AND GET OUT OF HERE!
IT HURTS!
SORRY, BUT I CAN'T GIVE YOU ANY PAINKILLERS WITHOUT THE INTERROGATOR'S PERMISSION.
WANT SOME MEDS? YOU'RE GONNA HAVE TO TELL US A LITTLE ABOUT THE OTHER DETAINEES.

They'd often ask us to tell on the other prisoners and say we were together in Afghanistan. Some detainees played the game. There was a Yemeni named YASIN BASARDAH. He must have been about 29. If they put him in a cell next to yours, he'd talk to you, ask you questions, so as to mix true and false information.

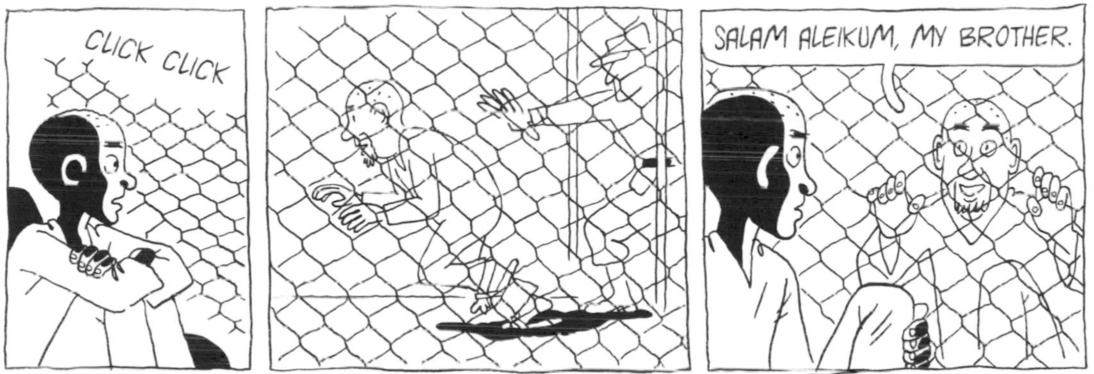
CLICK CLICK
SALAM ALEIKUM, MY BROTHER.

I know he told an interrogator I was an al-Qaida member. He said that about dozens of prisoners. In return, he was getting Coke and pizzas.

After a while, everyone knew it. Some brothers used to spit in his face.

I heard he was released after me and sent to Spain.

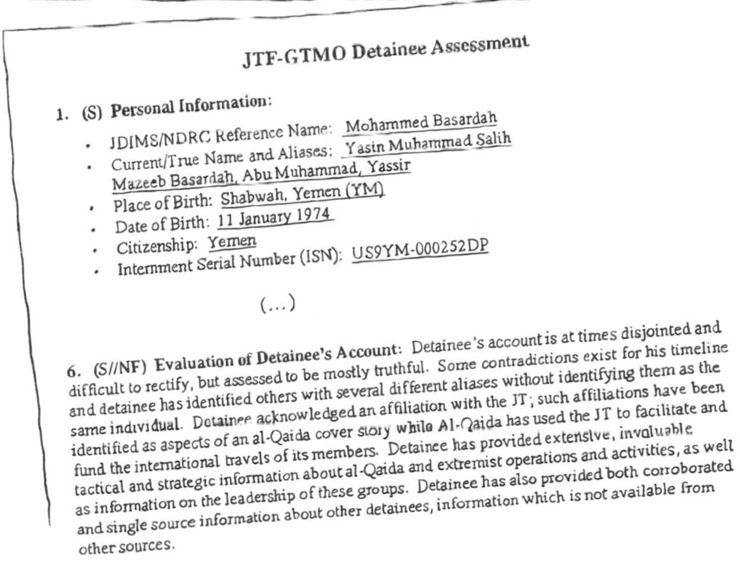

JTF-GTMO Detainee Assessment

1. (S) **Personal Information:**
   - JDIMS/NDRC Reference Name: Mohammed Basardah
   - Current/True Name and Aliases: Yasin Muhammad Salih Mazeeb Basardah, Abu Muhammad, Yassir
   - Place of Birth: Shabwah, Yemen (YM)
   - Date of Birth: 11 January 1974
   - Citizenship: Yemen
   - Internment Serial Number (ISN): US9YM-000252DP

(...)

6. (S//NF) **Evaluation of Detainee's Account:** Detainee's account is at times disjointed and difficult to rectify, but assessed to be mostly truthful. Some contradictions exist for his timeline and detainee has identified others with several different aliases without identifying them as the same individual. Detainee acknowledged an affiliation with the JT; such affiliations have been identified as aspects of an al-Qaida cover story while Al-Qaida has used the JT to facilitate and fund the international travels of its members. Detainee has provided extensive, invaluable tactical and strategic information about al-Qaida and extremist operations and activities, as well as information on the leadership of these groups. Detainee has also provided both corroborated and single source information about other detainees, information which is not available from other sources.

MOHAMMED, I KNOW YOU'RE INNOCENT, BUT I'M JUST DOING MY JOB. I'VE GOT KIDS TO FEED. I CAN'T AFFORD TO LOSE MY JOB.

THIS IS NO JOB, WHAT YOU'RE DOING HERE. IT'S A CRIME. SOONER OR LATER, YOU'LL PAY FOR THIS... EVEN IF ONLY IN THE AFTERLIFE!

I'M LIKE A MACHINE. I ASK YOU WHAT THEY TELL ME TO ASK, AND PASS ON YOUR ANSWERS. I DON'T CARE WHAT THEY ARE.

DON'T MAKE THIS HARDER THAN IT HAS TO BE. THERE ARE NO LAWYERS HERE. NO ONE CARES ABOUT YOU.

WE KNOW YOU WERE UP TO NO GOOD IN SUDAN.

I'VE NEVER BEEN THERE.

I KNOW. BUT IF YOU COOPERATE, I'LL BRING YOU PIZZAS AND MCDONALD'S.

I KNOW THE FOOD HERE IS BAD.

The food was inedible. One day, they gave us army rations with pork in them. It said "vegetarian" on the label, but inside, on the can, it said "pork". Some of the older brothers noticed.

LISTEN UP, EVERYONE! THERE'S PORK INSIDE! DON'T EAT IT!

YOU'RE NOT IN A MUSLIM COUNTRY! THIS IS ALL YOU'RE GETTING!

We all threw the food against the fences.

WE BROUGHT YOU SOME BREAKFUCKST.

WE'RE WITH THE F.B.I. WE'RE HERE TO ASK YOU SOME QUESTIONS.

FIRST OF ALL, WE'D LIKE TO KNOW WHAT YOU WERE DOING IN AFGHANISTAN.

YOU'D BETTER COOPERATE WITH US, SON. WE AT THE F.B.I. HAVE RULES WE HAVE TO FOLLOW. WHEN DETAINEES COOPERATE, WE TREAT THEM WELL. BUT IF YOU DON'T TALK, WE WON'T HAVE ANY CHOICE BUT TO TURN YOU OVER TO THE ARMY FOR INTERROGATION.

AND I DON'T THINK THEY'LL BRING YOU CHEESEBURGERS AND COFFEE.

WHO GAVE YOU THE MONEY TO GO TO AFGHANISTAN?

I'M THROUGH HERE.

HEY, MOTHERFUCKER! THOSE PEOPLE ARE AGENTS OF THE F.B.I.! THEY CAME SPECIALLY FROM WASHINGTON, D.C. TO ASK YOU QUESTIONS, AND YOU GAVE 'EM THE SILENT TREATMENT! YOU WANT ME TO DO THE ASKING INSTEAD?

CAPTAIN, IF YOU KEEP SHOUTING LIKE THAT, YOU'LL LOSE YOUR VOICE.

FUCK! GUARDS, CHAIN HIM UP TIGHT!

Another time:

WE KNOW YOU WERE WORKING WITH AL-QAIDA IN LONDON IN 1993. YOU WERE PART OF A CLANDESTINE CELL LED BY ABU QATADA AL-MASRI.

ARE YOU SURE?

LOOK: 1993.

YOU SHOULD BE BE SMART AND SAY 1998 OR 1999. IN 1993, I WAS SIX.

HA HA HA

Another time:

I'D LIKE YOU TO MEET SOMEONE TODAY.

HELLO...

IF YOU COOPERATE, YOU'LL GET TO SLEEP WITH ME.

After 5 minutes, maybe 10, she left. This happened a couple of times.

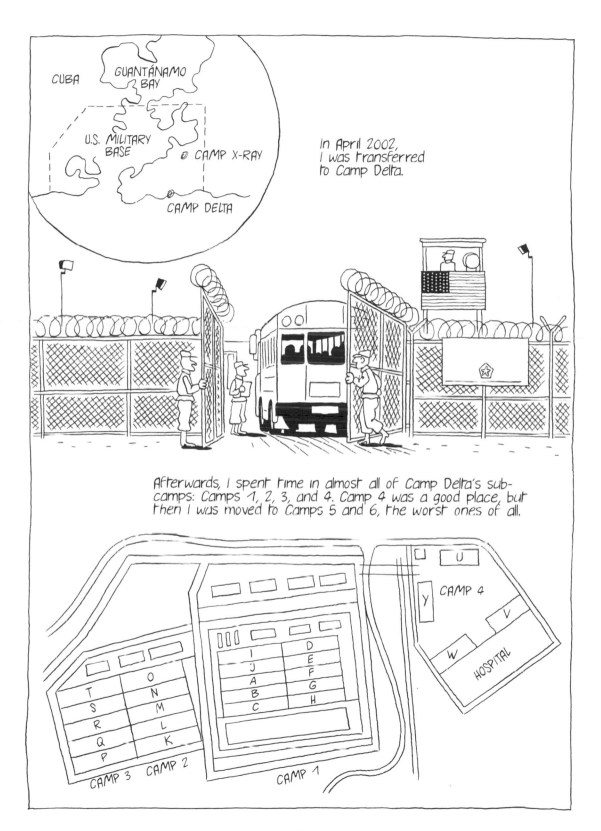

CUBA GUANTÁNAMO BAY

U.S. MILITARY BASE

CAMP X-RAY

CAMP DELTA

In April 2002, I was transferred to Camp Delta.

Afterwards, I spent time in almost all of Camp Delta's sub-camps: Camps 1, 2, 3, and 4. Camp 4 was a good place, but then I was moved to Camps 5 and 6, the worst ones of all.

CAMP 4

HOSPITAL

U

Y

W

V

T
S
R
Q
P

O
N
M
L
K

I
J
A
B
C

D
E
F
G
H

CAMP 3   CAMP 2   CAMP 1

At X-Ray, every day there was fighting, violence, pepper spray. Because it was the beginning, they'd only just opened Guantánamo. There was no such thing as a normal day. Normal life was Camp Delta.

You woke up in the morning around five, and prayed.

In fact, you weren't sure of the time because there were no watches, no clocks anywhere. The only way you could tell the time was from looking at the sun. But when it was cloudy, you couldn't see the sun. You could only guess at the time from when the guards ate, or when the night shift came on.

Sometimes we did our midday prayers at 4 p.m.

WHAT TIME IS IT?

TIME TO PRAY?

NO IDEA.

When we prayed, the guards made fun of us. They made us stay on our knees. Sometimes they beat us.

After we woke, we got breakfast. Bad milk and bad eggs, every day, which gave us stomach problems.

Most of the brothers didn't eat.

At 10 a.m., it was time for class. I asked the brothers who spoke English to teach me some new words. We'd go over the words from the day before.

CAT

CAT

My teachers were JAMAL, a Ugandan, and SHAKER AAMER, my best friend at Guantánamo.

DOG

DOG

SHUT UP!

BIRD

BIRD

SHUT UP!

CLONG

Some others were learning French.

WA-ZO

WA-ZO

SHUT UP!

In the beginning, the guards would punish us for trying to hold classes. When the guards noticed someone teaching me words, they'd move one of us. Because I got moved so often, I learned more English words, even if they were bad ones.

SHIT

FUCK

ASSHOLE

FUCK

I learned the soldiers' English.

I used soap to secretly write at least three new English words a day on the walls.

DOG
CAT
FATHER
MOTHER
SUN

That's how I learned English.

At X-Ray, we had fleas, lice, and no way to wash. Showers were once every three months. At Delta, there was a sink, but no soap. I managed to steal some and hide it under the door. Some good guards also gave me soap.

According to the camp's rules, or S.O.P. (Standard Operating Procedures), we were allowed two showers each week.

➡

4002. SHOWERS AND RECREATION: The following schedule will be utilized for shower and recreation call.

	DAY SHIFT	SWING SHIFT
MONDAY	UNITS 1-8	UNITS 9-16
TUESDAY	UNITS 17-24	UNITS 25-32
WEDNESDAY	UNITS 33-40	UNITS 41-48
THURSDAY	UNITS 1-8	UNITS 9-16
FRIDAY	UNITS 17-24	UNITS 25-32
SATURDAY	UNITS 33-40	UNITS 41-48
SUNDAY	NONE	NONE

1. Showers and recreation call will be conducted in conjunction with each other. The Block NCO will be responsible for ensuring each Detainee receives showers and recreation twice per week unless they are on discipline measures that include no recreation.
2. Each Detainee will be allowed 20 minutes for recreation. Immediately after recreation he will be allowed 5 minutes to shower. If the Detainee desires to shave his body hair he will be allowed an additional 5 minutes.

The shower was supposed to last 5 minutes, but some guards made you stop as soon as you'd soaped up.

TIME'S UP!

!

We'd talk to each other until 11, and then it was lunchtime.

Sometimes some undercooked rice, with a piece of bread. We had no fish or meat at first, only some vegetables. Just enough to keep you alive. Sometimes a cup filled with dried dates was all we got for lunch.

I was skinny, no more than 90 pounds, and I kept losing weight. Many of us were sick and kept throwing up because the food was so bad. The guards drove them to the hospital.

There was nothing to do after lunch.

At 1 p.m., 3 p.m., and 6 p.m., we prayed. I did a lot of push-ups, sit-ups, and running on the spot. If you didn't do anything, your knees started to hurt.

At night, we'd try to sleep, but the guards would switch all the lights on and bring in big vacuum cleaners to make a lot of noise. Sometimes, they'd play music very loud.

FUCK YOU, I WON'T DO WHAT YOU TELL ME!!

I didn't know what kind of music it was, but I understood that the words were bad words.

FUCK YOU, I WON'T DO WHAT YOU TELL ME!! FUCK YOU, I WON'T DO WHAT YOU TELL ME!!! MOTHER FUCKER!!! UGH!!!...

AND NOW YOU DO WHAT THEY TOLD YA, NOW YOU'RE UNDER CONTROL...*

* "Killing in the Name", by Rage Against the Machine. The band protested against the use of their music at Guantánamo. Other musicians approved the use of theirs.

Some detainees were singled out:

GET UP!

NO SLEEP

WAKE UP!

FUCK YOUR GOD, FUCK YOU!!

(DEICIDE)

The guards would wake them up all the time, or keep them from sleeping by moving them from their cells every hour.

DETAINEE, MOVE!

I'M ON THE HIGHWAY TO HELL!...

(AC/DC)

They called this the "Frequent Flyer Program".

They did it to me for thirty days. It was exhausting.

NO FOOD

NO EXERCISE

NO TALKING

HIT ME BABY ONE MORE TIME!

(BRITNEY SPEARS)

When it wasn't too noisy, but I still couldn't sleep, I'd talk with my neighbor in the next cell over about the past, our families, or history.

There were no books in Guantánamo. Only toward the end did our interrogators bring us some.

In Medina, I'd liked history books. My parents had a few books, and I'd also go to the library in the Prophet's Mosque.

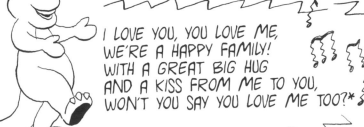

I LOVE YOU, YOU LOVE ME, WE'RE A HAPPY FAMILY! WITH A GREAT BIG HUG AND A KISS FROM ME TO YOU, WON'T YOU SAY YOU LOVE ME TOO?*

*Theme of the children's T.V. show *Barney & Friends*, perhaps the most frequently broadcast song in Guantánamo.

That was the music in Guantánamo. Me, I'd sing my own songs. I'd make up lyrics, in Arabic or in English. And other detainees would sing along with me. My biggest hit was called:

At X-Ray, they gave us two buckets, one with water for drinking and washing, and the other for pissing and shitting in. For the second bucket, they told us to call out "Number 1" or "Number 2", and they'd come and take it away. No. 1 was the code for piss and No. 2 for shit.

At Delta, we didn't have buckets anymore, so we'd throw shit with a plastic cup.

JTF-GTMO Detainee Assessment

1. (S) **Personal Information:**
    - JDIMS/NDRC Reference Name: <u>Yousef Abkir Salih al-Qarani</u>
    - Current/True Name and Aliases: <u>Muhammad Hamid Ali al-Qarani,</u> <u>Abu Ali, Ali Hassan Muhammad Hamid, Abu Dujana,</u> <u>Fadel, Khourbali, Yusuf Abkar Salih, Yusuf al-Chadi,</u>
    - Place of Birth: <u>Medina, Saudi Arabia (SA)</u>
    - Date of Birth: <u>1981</u>
    - Citizenship: <u>Chad (CD)</u>
      Internment Serial Number (ISN): <u>US9CD-000269DP</u>

(...)

c. (S//NF) **Detainee's Conduct:** Detainee is assessed as a **HIGH** threat from a detention perspective. His overall behavior has been non-compliant and hostile towards the guard force and staff. He currently has 385 Reports of Disciplinary Infraction listed in DIMS with the most recent occurring on 1 April 2008, when he was in possession of two, one inch screws from the ceiling light. He has 60 Reports of Disciplinary Infraction for assault with the most recent occurring on 17 March 2008, when he threw feces on the guard force. Other incidents for which he has been disciplined include inciting and participating in mass disturbances, failure to follow guard instructions/camp rules, inappropriate use of bodily fluids, unauthorized communications, exposing his genitals, damage to government property, attempted assaults, provoking words and gestures, and possession of food and non-weapon type contraband. In 2007, he had a total of 192 Reports of Disciplinary Infraction and 71 so far in 2008.

They called me a troublemaker. There was a big sign on my door:

NO CONVERSATION WITH 269

269 was my number, but I didn't like being called 269.

HEY, 269!

I'M NOT A NUMBER!

Since I wouldn't answer to "269", they started calling me "Chris Tucker" instead. Have you seen the movie *Rush Hour*, with Jackie Chan and Chris Tucker, a black actor?

HEY, CHRIS!

WASSUP, MAN?

HOW ABOUT YOU? WHAT'S YOUR NAME?

FORGET IT.

The guards' names were written on their uniforms, but most of them covered it up with tape.

The guards didn't cover their names at first. I remember one called Smith. The reason I remember him is he was a very bad guy, the worst guard I saw in Guantánamo. He was blond — it was the first time I'd seen so many people with blond hair and blue eyes.

SMITH   U.S. ARMY

CRACK

CRACK

He was a big, strong guy, and he was always beating on us. Whenever we saw him, we knew it was going to be a bad day.

JACKIE CHAN   CHRIS TUCKER

RUSH HOUR

Later on, most American soldiers I saw covered up their names. They were scared, or ashamed. So we gave them nicknames. Everyone had a nickname in Guantánamo.

I used to ask the good guards the names of the bad guards, and where they came from. I remember one, also with blond hair and blue eyes, who was in his twenties.

HEY, HONKIE! I KNOW YOUR NAME AND I KNOW WHERE YOU'RE FROM. SOMEDAY WHEN I GET OUT OF HERE, I'M GONNA KICK YOUR ASS!

HOW COULD YOU KNOW MY NAME?

He checked his name tag. Had he forgotten to cover it up? No.

I KNOW YOUR NAME IS ███████ █████ AND YOU COME FROM ███████...

DON'T SAY THAT OUT LOUD!

NO CONVERSATION WITH

I KNOW YOUR HOMETOWN. I KNOW YOUR FAMILY. I KNOW ALL THE DETAILS!

Actually, all I knew was his name and his hometown.

WHO TOLD YOU?

I WON'T TELL YOU. BUT SOMEDAY, I'M GETTING OUT OF HERE, AND THEN YOU'LL SEE.

I DON'T CARE.

He started pacing around the cell block. I don't think he slept that night.

The next day he came back.

BROTHER!

OH, SO I'M YOUR BROTHER NOW...

I KNOW I'VE BEEN A BAD MAN. ACTUALLY, I'VE BEEN HAVING A LOT OF PROBLEMS AT HOME. BUT I'VE GOT NO BEEF WITH YOU.

NO CONVERSATION WITH 269

The guards were cowards.

Most stayed one year. November was the time for their relief. I talked a lot with the newcomers.

HEY YOU!

?

WE DON'T KNOW EACH OTHER. I KNOW YOU'VE RULES TO OBSERVE...

BUT WE'RE HUMAN BEINGS JUST LIKE YOU, NOT ANIMALS. DON'T BELIEVE ALL THE BRAINWASHING. EVERYTHING THEY'VE SAID ABOUT US. I DON'T WANT TO BE HERE, YOU DON'T WANT TO BE HERE, WHY MAKE LIFE HARDER? DO UNTO OTHERS AS YOU WOULD HAVE THEM DO UNTO YOU.

YOU'RE NOT HERE TO JUDGE ME. THINK ABOUT IT!

That's what I always told them. Some listened, others didn't.

SHUT UP!

I talked to the guards about everything: how they lived, their jobs at the camp, their life back in the States. I'd picked up their accent, and many thought I'd been to the U.S., or even believed I was American.

In the morning, I'd ask the guards who the S.O.G.* was that day, and I'd know if the day was going to be good or bad, long or short.
*S.O.G.: Sergeant of the Guard, commanding a guard unit.

Once, one of our brothers was badly beaten in front of us. His chin was all bloody. I sat in my room and didn't speak to anyone all day. During the night shift, one of the good guards, a black guy from Louisiana, came to see me.

We called him Mike Tyson because he was a boxer. He used to fist bump me hello through the bars.

WASSUP, CHRIS? WHAT'S WRONG?

Finally, I talked.

YOU SEE WHAT THEY DID TO HIM? I'D UNDERSTAND IF HE'D DONE SOMETHING WRONG, BUT HE DIDN'T DO ANYTHING!

BROTHER, LOOK AT ME! HOW LONG YOU BEEN HERE WITH THE AMERICANS?

FOUR YEARS.

ME, I'M 27, BROTHER. I'VE BEEN IN THE SAME SHIT FOR 27 YEARS!

I KNOW HOW IT IS. THEY THREW MY BROTHER IN JAIL FOR NO REASON, INSTEAD OF A WHITE GUY. MOST OF THE PEOPLE IN JAIL IN THE U.S. ARE BLACK, YOU KNOW.

MY GRANDFATHER AND MY GREAT-GRANDFATHER WERE IN THE SAME SITUATION YOU'RE IN NOW.

US BLACK FOLK HAVE BEEN TREATED LIKE YOU.

He talked to me for two hours, until his boss came and he left. He had helped me a lot. He was a good guy.

We talked regularly for a year. He asked me a lot of questions about Islam.

BEFORE I CAME TO GUANTÁNAMO, THE MEDIA TOLD ME MUSLIMS HATE US BECAUSE OF OUR WAY OF LIFE, BECAUSE OF FREEDOM AND DEMOCRACY.

BUT WHEN I CAME HERE, I SAW THAT YOU MUSLIMS RESPECT EACH OTHER AND HAVE NO HATE FOR PEOPLE OF OTHER RELIGIONS. I SAW YOU READING THE QURAN AND CALLING EVERYONE TO PRAYER. YOU'RE THE YOUNGEST AND THE ONLY BLACK GUY, AND THEY LISTEN TO YOU! THERE'S NO RACISM AMONG YOU!

IN THE PROPHET'S DAY, THE FIRST MUEZZIN, BILAL, WAS BLACK.

Sometimes he'd bring ice cream, chocolate bars, or chips from his own stash. He could've gotten fired for that. One night:

WASSUP, MAN?

HIDE THIS!

MAN, I'M LEAVING TONIGHT.

WHERE?

AMERICA!

I'LL NEVER SEE YOU AGAIN FOR THE REST OF MY LIFE, BUT SINCE COMING HERE, MY EYES HAVE BEEN OPENED. AS SOON AS I GET TO THE U.S., I'M GOING TO CONVERT TO ISLAM AND LEAVE THE ARMY.

I'LL NEVER FORGET YOU, TYSON.

GOOD LUCK, MY BROTHER!

He was the best of all the guards.

The good guards were often black or Latino, but there was also a black guy who was very bad. When he came, every one was scared, even the other guards. We called him "Pharaoh".*

I called him "Uncle Tom".*

*In reference to the bad Pharaoh, who, according to the Bible and the Quran, persecuted Moses and the Jews.

*In the U.S., a common insult toward black men who collaborate with white men, in reference to the novel *Uncle Tom's Cabin*.

He beat me many times, and called other guards over to beat me too.

WASSUP, UNCLE TOM?

YOU WANT A THRASHING?

But I didn't stop insulting him.

WASSUP, UNCLE TOM?

In the end, he started laughing.

When the bad guards saw us sad and sick, they were happy. And I didn't want that. Even after interrogations, when I got back to the block, I tried to keep smiling.

WHY ARE YOU LAUGHING?

I'M HAPPY!

HOW CAN YOU BE HAPPY? YOU'RE IN JAIL.

Because they thought I was generous, the brothers nicknamed me "Sunbul", "the ear of grain". It was a reference to the Sura of "The Cow", which says: "The parable of those who spend their wealth in the way of Allah is as the parable of a grain growing seven ears, in every ear a hundred grains."

I knew the Quran and the stories of the prophets. There was a lot of sadness in their stories. God was testing them. I believe that in Guantánamo, God was testing us, too. He was testing our patience.

In 2003, we were allowed to have a Quran. It was a medium-sized green Quran. I believe it was allowed for two reasons: to make the media think we were being treated well, and to make us angry when the Quran was disrespected.

I cleaned the Quran and put it back in its place. I wouldn't kick the Bible, ever. It's a holy book too. But when I saw people kicking the Quran, it made me sad. It's one of the more serious things Americans did to us. Something I never thought I'd see in my lifetime, before I became a prisoner. It happened several times. Sometimes they tore up the Quran, sometimes they threw it in the toilet.

There were some very nice small birds: yellow, red, and blue. I watched the ones that came the closest to my window; I could hear them singing.

One day I was sitting there, mad, sad, and angry — it was one of those days.

  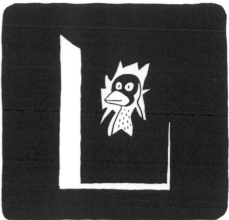

The guards had covered our windows with brown tape, to prevent daylight coming in from outside. A woodpecker came and pecked and pecked until it broke the tape and made a hole big as a coin.

The bird started doing it every day, and every day, the guards had to tape over the hole. This happened to a lot of windows. There are lots of woodpeckers in Cuba, but it was just this one bird. We called him Woody Woodpecker.

Sometimes, the guards left the holes alone for several days. I could see the cars, the soldiers, the sky, the sun... life outside.

When an officer came, we would complain about the bad guards.

IF YOU HAVE AN ISSUE WITH A GUARD, JUST GIVE ME HIS NAME.

BUT THE GUARDS COVER UP THEIR NAMES!

BETTER FIND A WAY TO IDENTIFY THEM.

COLONEL

Shaker Aamer, in his cell:

GIVE THE GUARDS NUMBERS, LIKE YOU DID WITH US!

We went on hunger strike, and they ended up giving the guards numbers.

Changing things was not easy. We always had to fight.

At first we had no choice. We put up with everything. In 2004, we started getting tougher.

Sometimes women did the searches at Camp X-Ray. We didn't like that at all.

They stopped using women to search us.

They'd also pat us down from belt to knee.

But they stopped that, too. We fought for that for days on end, months, even.

In 2004:

WE'RE TAKING YOU TO A PLACE WHERE WE'RE GOING TO TEACH YOU WHAT TO SAY.

CAMP DELTA

CAMP 5

CAMP ECHO

Camp 5 had just been built. I was among the first to be transferred there. They had moved maybe 40 detainees there to test it and conduct tough interrogations.

There's a movie, *Face/Off,** that I saw before I was arrested. Camp 5 was like the prison in that movie. All the doors were opened by computer, from a control room hidden behind two-way mirrors.

* Directed by JOHN WOO, with NICOLAS CAGE and JOHN TRAVOLTA.

The light was too bright, and stayed on 24 hours a day. One day, I got fed up and covered the lamp with my T-shirt. Everyone else started doing it too. The Americans punished me for that.

At Camp 5, no matter what you asked the guards, they said:

> ASK THE INTERROGATORS.

And whatever you asked the interrogators, they said:

> ASK THE GUARDS.

It happened when we asked to go outside (normally we had one hour in the rec yard twice a week) and to change our clothes (normally every Sunday)...

We spent three months in the same clothes, with no showers, no doctors, and no rec yard.

After three months, they let six or seven of us out in the yard. The rec yard was divided into individual cells, fully fenced:

We had one hour. When it was over:

> BROTHERS! EVER SINCE GETTING HERE, WE'VE NEVER GOTTEN ANYTHING WITHOUT A FIGHT. WHEN SOME GUARDS GOT HURT, THEY STOPPED MAKING NOISE AT NIGHT. THEN THEY ALLOWED US TO PRAY AS WE WISHED. NOW LET'S REFUSE TO GO BACK TO OUR CELLS!

> AND THEN?

> THEY'LL HIT US AND PEPPER SPRAY US. BUT WE HAVE TO GET THE ATTENTION OF THE HIGHER-UPS. EVEN IF THEY'RE ALREADY AWARE, THEY'LL HAVE TO REPORT IT TO THE PENTAGON.

There was a Yemeni among us whose back was already injured. We convinced him to go back to his cell so he wouldn't get hurt even worse.

We stayed outside for five hours instead of one. They didn't want any trouble. They didn't want to call the team, they let us do what we wanted.

When it was over:

YOU'LL BE THE LAST ONE OUT!

WE'RE ONLY PUNISHING THE RINGLEADERS. 269, GIVE US YOUR CLOTHES AND PUT ON THESE SHORTS.

Camp 5 had four cell blocks: Alpha, Bravo, Charlie, and Delta. At first, I was in Alpha upper, Cell 2-13. Then they took me to Charlie lower, Cell 111.

There was nothing inside the cell: no mat, no blanket. It was completely empty.

SALAM ALEIKUM!

ALEIKUM SALAM!

SUNBUL, IS THAT YOU? WHAT ARE YOU DOING HERE?

WHAT HAPPENED?

There were six brothers in nearby cells. One of them was Shaker Aamer.

Shaker Aamer was born in Medina, like me. We spoke the same Arabic. He was from one of the richest families in Medina; I'd heard their name before. He had long been living in London and married a British wife. In 2001, with their kids, they had moved to Afghanistan for a humanitarian organization. Shaker had been arrested there.*

I don't know what Shaker was doing in Afghanistan. There are some questions you didn't ask in Guantánamo. Some prisoners openly admitted they were Taliban or members of al-Qaida, but I don't think Shaker was either. I believe that when you're in prison, you find out who your real friends are.

I also had close friends who were younger than Shaker, like Ahmed from Yemen, and Fawzi, from Kuwait. I didn't ask them if they were with al-Qaida, but we'd talk about the same things, laugh at the same jokes.

But when I needed an advice, I always asked an elder like Shaker. He's the one who really helped me in Guantánamo. He really looked after me.

Sometimes I wouldn't see him for months, but I still got his advice, through guards or, later, through lawyers. We were the same. He was my homeboy, my homie. He was my number one, the best friend I had!

* Shaker Aamer was never charged with any crime and was never given the right to a trial. In 2007, the U.S. government cleared him for release. But he was only freed in 2015, after 14 years in detention.

Suddenly, I heard a noise behind my cell door. The slot opened, and I saw guards looking in at me.

SCREEEEECH

The Team!

The Team. That was five guards wearing helmets, elbow pads, kneepads, and gloves, like the riot police you see on T.V.*

*The Team was also called the "Immediate Reaction Force".

When they came, the first one would bang his shield on the door to scare you.

BOOM
BOOM

DETAINEE! LIE DOWN!

CONTROL, OPEN THE DOOR!

There's a rule in their rulebook, their S.O.P.: it says that if you comply and lie face down, hands and feet crossed behind your back, they won't spray you with pepper spray. They just have to come into the cell, shackle you, and take you out. But actually, even when we lay down, they sprayed us anyway. So we never lay down.

"The Number One Man is responsible for pinning the detainee with the shield and for securing the head."

"The Number Two Man is responsible for securing the detainee's right arm and for shackling the detainee's wrist."

"The Number Three Man is responsible for securing the detainee's left arm... He will assist the Number Two Man in shackling the detainee's wrist."

"The Number Four Man is responsible for securing the detainee's right leg. He will also have the leg irons."

"The Number Five Man is also the Team Leader. He is responsible for all actions of the team. He will give all verbal commands to the team. He is responsible for securing the detainee's left leg. He will assist the Number Four Man in shackling of the detainee's ankles."

Each member of the team holds on to the man in front of him. If something happens to one of them, he moves up. Also, there's always a guy with pepper spray, another one outside filming with a camera, and a medic in case someone gets hurt.

I knew the S.O.P. because a good guard had lent me the book in 2003, in Delta. He was a black guy, 28 or 29; I called him "Chocolate City" because he had told me he was from Washington, D.C.* He would secretly lend me the S.O.P. for a few hours, or even read it to me — at the time I couldn't read English very well.

* Chocolate City is one of Washington, D.C.'s nicknames, because of the town's significant African-American population.

The Team was at my door. I could see their faces: it was all guys who hated me. The good guards would warn us when their turn came. They'd say they'd take care not to hit too hard.

HEY, IT'S THE AMERICAN FOOTBALL TEAM!

269!

WHAT DO YOU WANT?

WE WANNA GIVE YOU A SHOT!

WHY?

TO CALM YOU DOWN.

I DON'T NEED IT, I'M CALM.

YOU HAVE NO CHOICE!

Shaker Aamer:

HEY! CRIMINALS! WHAT ARE YOU GUYS UP TO?

I was ready for a little fight.

YES OR NO?

NO!

They sent the pepper spray through the slot.

SHIT!

I tried to keep my mouth shut. If you breathe through your mouth, you'll pass out.

CONTROL, OPEN CHARLIE CELL 111!

OPENING CHARLIE CELL 111?

YES, CHARLIE 111!

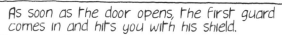
As soon as the door opens, the first guard comes in and hits you with his shield.

I passed out right away.

When I woke up, I was back in Alpha 213. My room was empty. The A.C. was on and it was very cold; I was shivering.

I felt very tired. I couldn't stand up. I crawled over to the door. I could hear voices talking.

SALAM ALEIKUM!

ALEIKUM SALAM!

They seemed happy to hear me.

HOW ARE YOU? ARE YOU HURT?

WHY DO YOU ASK?

I'd forgotten what had happened. I thought I had just come back from the rec yard.

DID YOU FINISH THE DHUHR* PRAYER?

* Midday prayer.

WE'VE BEEN CALLING YOUR NAME FOR THREE DAYS!

WHAT DAY IS IT?

SUNDAY. YOU'VE BEEN ASLEEP SINCE FRIDAY.

I remembered the injection.

M.P.!

We called guards from the Military Police M.P.s, those from the Marines M.A.s.

WASSUP, MAN?

OPEN THE WINDOW, I CAN'T HEAR YOU.

When they punish you or beat you, they want to see if you give up or not. After the injection, they thought I was calm and I'd just come to them nicely and ask them for clothes.

74

As soon as he opened up, I grabbed his whistle.

WHEEEE

A whistle means an emergency. All the guards come.

WHEEEE WHEEEE

PLEASE GIVE ME THE WHISTLE. DON'T MAKE ME LOOK STUPID!

WHEEEE

ALPHA 213 TOOK A WHISTLE! CODE YELLOW, CODE YELLOW!

NO RADIO! NO POINT CALLING EVERYONE OVER!

Normally Code Yellow meant there was a risk of death. But that guard just used it to call other guards. Code Red was more serious; it was for when somebody wasn't responding, or was maybe dead.

WHEEEE

GET UP STAND UP STAND UP FOR YOUR RIGHTS!

WHEEEE

GET UP, STAND UP, DON'T GIVE UP THE FIGHT!

Most of the guards were bursting out laughing, covering their mouths with their hands. They didn't want their superiors to see them and punish them. Then the S.O.G. came.

This S.O.G. was a Mexican dude from Texas, maybe 45 years old. Other S.O.G.s wouldn't come to me, because I'd spit on them. But he was very cool with me. He taught me "un, dos, tres, cuatro" — if he was on duty, I never had any problems.

COME ON, CHRIS! WHY ARE YOU DOING THIS TO ME? DIDN'T YOU KNOW I'M WORKING TODAY? GIVE ME THE WHISTLE...

LOOK, I'VE BEEN OUT OF IT FOR THREE DAYS. I DON'T EVEN HAVE ANY CLOTHES.

CONTROL? S.O.G.!

CONTROL! GO AHEAD!

269 IS ASKING FOR HIS CLOTHES. GIVE HIM HIS CLOTHES BACK!

STAND BY, S.O.G.!

He stayed with me for fifteen minutes, chatting.

CHRIS, YOU KNOW I LIKE YOU BEST OF ALL, 'CAUSE YOU'RE NOT SCARED AND YOU STAND UP FOR YOUR RIGHTS. LOOK, I DON'T AGREE WITH ALL THIS SHIT, AND I KNOW YOU'RE INNOCENT... BUT WHAT CAN I DO?

Lots of brothers had these injections. Some slept for six days.

In Camp 5, I was making trouble every day, because I had nothing else to do. To calm me down, they put me next to Shaker's cell, because they knew I'd listen to him. I stayed quiet for two weeks...

PUT YOUR T-SHIRT BACK, 269!

IT ITCHES TOO MUCH, 'CAUSE OF THE HEAT!

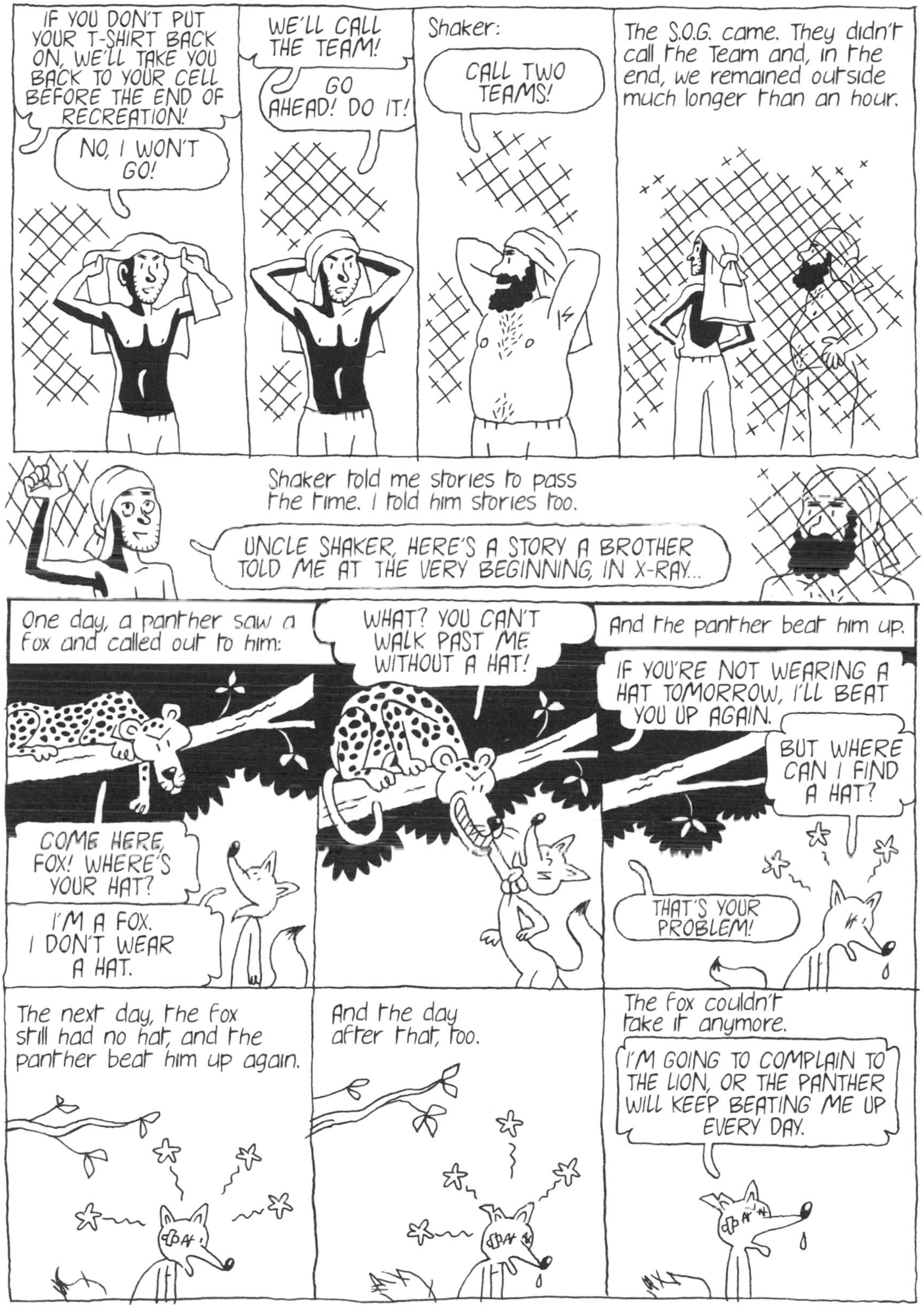
IF YOU DON'T PUT YOUR T-SHIRT BACK ON, WE'LL TAKE YOU BACK TO YOUR CELL BEFORE THE END OF RECREATION!
NO, I WON'T GO!
WE'LL CALL THE TEAM!
GO AHEAD! DO IT!
Shaker:
CALL TWO TEAMS!
The S.O.G. came. They didn't call the Team and, in the end, we remained outside much longer than an hour.
Shaker told me stories to pass the time. I told him stories too.
UNCLE SHAKER, HERE'S A STORY A BROTHER TOLD ME AT THE VERY BEGINNING, IN X-RAY...
One day, a panther saw a fox and called out to him:
COME HERE, FOX! WHERE'S YOUR HAT?
I'M A FOX. I DON'T WEAR A HAT.
WHAT? YOU CAN'T WALK PAST ME WITHOUT A HAT!
And the panther beat him up.
IF YOU'RE NOT WEARING A HAT TOMORROW, I'LL BEAT YOU UP AGAIN.
BUT WHERE CAN I FIND A HAT?
THAT'S YOUR PROBLEM!
The next day, the fox still had no hat, and the panther beat him up again.
And the day after that, too.
The fox couldn't take it anymore.
I'M GOING TO COMPLAIN TO THE LION, OR THE PANTHER WILL KEEP BEATING ME UP EVERY DAY.

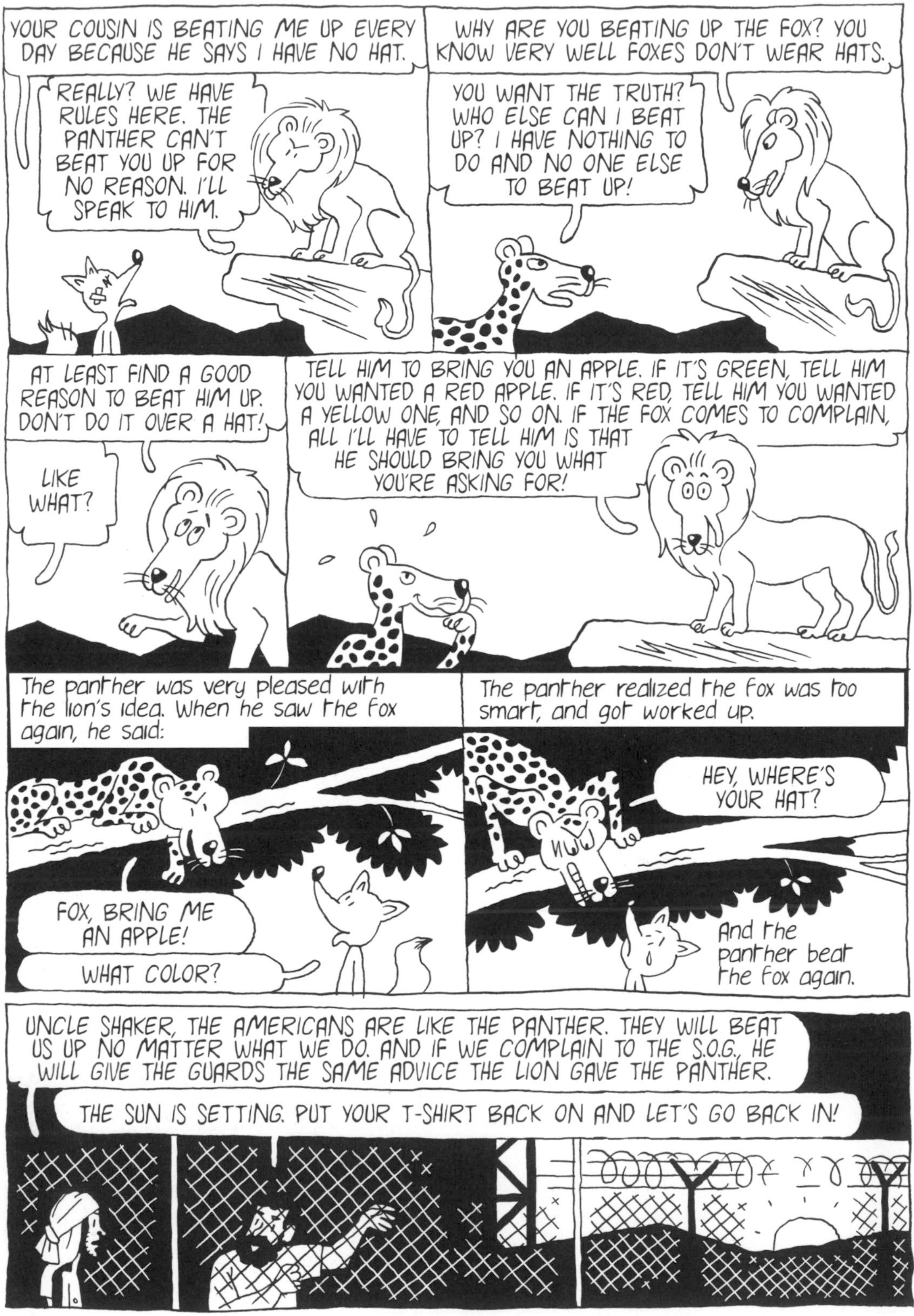

YOUR COUSIN IS BEATING ME UP EVERY DAY BECAUSE HE SAYS I HAVE NO HAT.
REALLY? WE HAVE RULES HERE. THE PANTHER CAN'T BEAT YOU UP FOR NO REASON. I'LL SPEAK TO HIM.
WHY ARE YOU BEATING UP THE FOX? YOU KNOW VERY WELL FOXES DON'T WEAR HATS.
YOU WANT THE TRUTH? WHO ELSE CAN I BEAT UP? I HAVE NOTHING TO DO AND NO ONE ELSE TO BEAT UP!
AT LEAST FIND A GOOD REASON TO BEAT HIM UP. DON'T DO IT OVER A HAT!
LIKE WHAT?
TELL HIM TO BRING YOU AN APPLE. IF IT'S GREEN, TELL HIM YOU WANTED A RED APPLE. IF IT'S RED, TELL HIM YOU WANTED A YELLOW ONE, AND SO ON. IF THE FOX COMES TO COMPLAIN, ALL I'LL HAVE TO TELL HIM IS THAT HE SHOULD BRING YOU WHAT YOU'RE ASKING FOR!
The panther was very pleased with the lion's idea. When he saw the fox again, he said:
FOX, BRING ME AN APPLE!
WHAT COLOR?
The panther realized the fox was too smart, and got worked up.
HEY, WHERE'S YOUR HAT?
And the panther beat the fox again.
UNCLE SHAKER, THE AMERICANS ARE LIKE THE PANTHER. THEY WILL BEAT US UP NO MATTER WHAT WE DO. AND IF WE COMPLAIN TO THE S.O.G., HE WILL GIVE THE GUARDS THE SAME ADVICE THE LION GAVE THE PANTHER.
THE SUN IS SETTING. PUT YOUR T-SHIRT BACK ON AND LET'S GO BACK IN!

The more we fought for our rights, the more problems we had with our health. We went on hunger strikes all together. The biggest one was in 2005.

I held out for twenty days. Shaker was one of the leaders. He negotiated with the colonel in charge of the camp, who agreed to improve detention conditions, and we stopped striking.

Colonel BUMGARNER

But a week later, they beat up Hisham, a brother from Tunisia, very badly. And we went back on strike.

HISHAM BIN ALI BIN AMOR SLITI

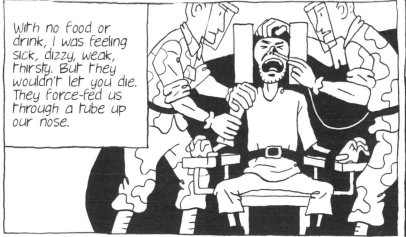

With no food or drink, I was feeling sick, dizzy, weak, thirsty. But they wouldn't let you die. They force-fed us through a tube up our nose.

After a month, Shaker was put in solitary confinement. He stayed in solitary for over a year.

It was a time when they had instituted a lot of stupid rules. Don't talk to your neighbor, don't stand up on your bed, don't sit close to your cell door, and when you go to the toilet, don't cover up. The guards, even female ones, came to watch and laugh at us.

I always told my brothers to cover themselves or cover the window before using the toilet. When the guards wouldn't let me do that, I'd piss on the door, and they had to clean it up. All the brothers started doing that. The block stank! Then another incident occurred.

COULD YOU PLEASE BRING ME MY LEGAL DOCUMENTS?

O.K., IT'S YOUR RIGHT.

Later:

269, YOUR DOC...

SMASH

ECHO BLOCK

I was moved to Seg - segregation. They made noise with vacuum cleaners, and there was no way of talking to anyone. When you were allowed out into the rec yard, you had to go alone. And there were even more deprivations.

NO BREAKFAST TODAY, THE GALLEY DIDN'T BRING FOOD. IF YOU WANT TO EAT TOMORROW, TALK TO YOUR INTERROGATOR!

In Seg, every day, and even at night, you got the Team and pepper spray. There was a lot of beating and my body was burning because of the spray. The A.C. was ice cold, and they poured a stinking chemical into it on the pretext of cleaning it.

You couldn't breathe.

Many detainees tried to commit suicide, but I don't think any succeeded. Six brothers did die. We were told they killed themselves. I knew them, they were always hopeful — it's so hard to believe that those six, of all people, killed themselves.

*The official inquiry claimed that Zaharani had hung himself with his sheets, together with two other detainees. Independent counter-inquiries concluded the three probably died as a result of torture.

MUSLIM BURIAL*
(Side View)

Figure 16-1

* Sketch taken from Guantánamo's Standard Operating Procedures (S.O.P.) manual.

I also thought of killing myself. I wondered how to do it.
Several times, I tried to cut my wrists on the metal of the door.

I tried to hang myself by tying my clothes together.
Guards intervened and changed my cell.

Shrinks came and asked me why I was doing this.

I tried again, but this time I stopped myself.

I remembered a passage from the Quran...

"And do not kill yourselves. Indeed, Allah is to you ever Merciful. And whoever does this in transgression and injustice — then We will condemn him to fire. And that, for Allah, is easy."
Sura 4: 29-30

Hell, from an Islamic miniature.

... If you kill yourself, you go to hell. So I stopped thinking about suicide.

They moved me to Psych Block.

WELCOME TO PSYCH BLOCK!

WHEN DETAINEES LOSE THEIR MINDS, WE BRING THEM HERE.

They also used to take visitors there when they came to "tour" the camp...

LOOK...

NATIONAL GEOGRAPHIC

THEY HAVE A GOOD LIFE HERE. THEY GET WHATEVER THEY WANT.

LIAR!

TELL THE TRUTH! THEY BEAT US HERE!

?

AS I WAS SAYING...

THEY GET WHATEVER THEY WANT. LOOK WHAT THEY'VE GOT IN THEIR CELLS.

YES! COME AND LOOK WHAT I HAVE IN MY CELL!

CAN WE TAKE A PEEK?

SURE...

LOOK! WHERE ARE THE BOOKS AND THE NEWSPAPERS?

THIS GUY IS DISORDERLY. HE'S BEING PUNISHED.

IT'S NOT JUST ME! EVERYBODY HERE IS TREATED LIKE THIS! IS EVERYBODY DISORDERLY?!

Sometimes they'd beat me for talking like this. The block had 48 cells, including two segregation cells, one of them with no light. They'd put me in that one. It was so dark you couldn't see your own hand.

I was going crazy, banging my head on the wall.

In late 2006, they opened a new camp, Camp 6 — a bigger one than Camp 5.

CAMP 6 IS NICE. YOU'LL SEE. GENEVA CONVENTIONS ARE RESPECTED THERE. YOU'LL HAVE A BIG REC YARD, FOOTBALL, T.V.! YOU'RE GOING TO BE CHILLIN' LIKE A VILLAIN!

IF THAT'S TRUE, GREAT. IF NOT, LET'S GET READY FOR A FIGHT.

IT'LL ALL BE FINE! THEY'LL BE RESPECTING THE GENEVA CONVENTIONS!

JUST REMEMBER, AMERICANS HAVE ALWAYS LIED TO US...

DON'T SAY THAT! IT'LL BE ALRIGHT!

I'VE BEEN IN CAMP 5! WE HAVE TO STICK TOGETHER AND FIGHT FOR EVEN A LITTLE FREEDOM. WE'RE LIVING HERE...

WE HAVE TO MAKE OUR LIVES HERE BETTER.

CAMP 5

CAMP 6

In Camp 6, I made a lot of trouble. I'd provoke the guards and tell them to call the Team. Then they wouldn't call it!

If they saw that I was happy in one block, they'd move me to another. Even when I was happy in Segregation, they'd move me to regular. Once, I hit a guard.

And it worked. They didn't put me in Segregation. Well, sometimes it didn't work. Anyway, Camp 6 was like Camp 5: more segregated than Segregation in the other camps.

They didn't touch the A.C. all day. Then, when the night shift came on:

BROTHERS, LISTEN! LET'S COVER THE VENTS IN OUR CELLS WITH PAPER!

GOOD IDEA!

For an hour each day, we were allowed to see our legal documents and have paper to write letters. We had toothpaste, too, but it stank, so we didn't use it.

LET'S PASTE PAPER OVER THE A.C. WITH TOOTHPASTE AND WATER.

WILL IT WORK?

YES, I DID IT BEFORE IN CAMP 5.

We told the older brothers they didn't have to take part, because we knew we would get the Team. Seventeen out of twenty-four prisoners in the block did it. The same guard, "Piece-of-Shit", was on duty. He saw it.

269, TAKE IT DOWN!

IT'S SNOWING OUTSIDE. WE DON'T WANT THE SNOW TO GET IN!

CONTROL, THIS IS FOXTROT ONE!

GO AHEAD, FOXTROT ONE!

CELL 103'S COVERING THE A.C.!

NOT JUST ME! 102, 104, 105, 106...

AND ALSO 102, 104, 105, 106...

269!

MY NAME IS MOHAMMED!

WHY ARE YOU COVERING THE A.C.?

LISTEN, YOUR OWN BOOK, YOUR S.O.P., SAYS IT'S SUPPOSED TO BE 78°.

HOW DO YOU KNOW?

I KNOW THE RULES.

I'VE BEEN HERE SIX YEARS. IT'S BEEN THE SAME SHIT EVER SINCE I'VE BEEN HERE.

SAME WHAT? DON'T SAY "SHIT"!

I'M TALKING LIKE YOU.

IT'S 78°

NO, IT'S NOT.

CALL THE TEAM!

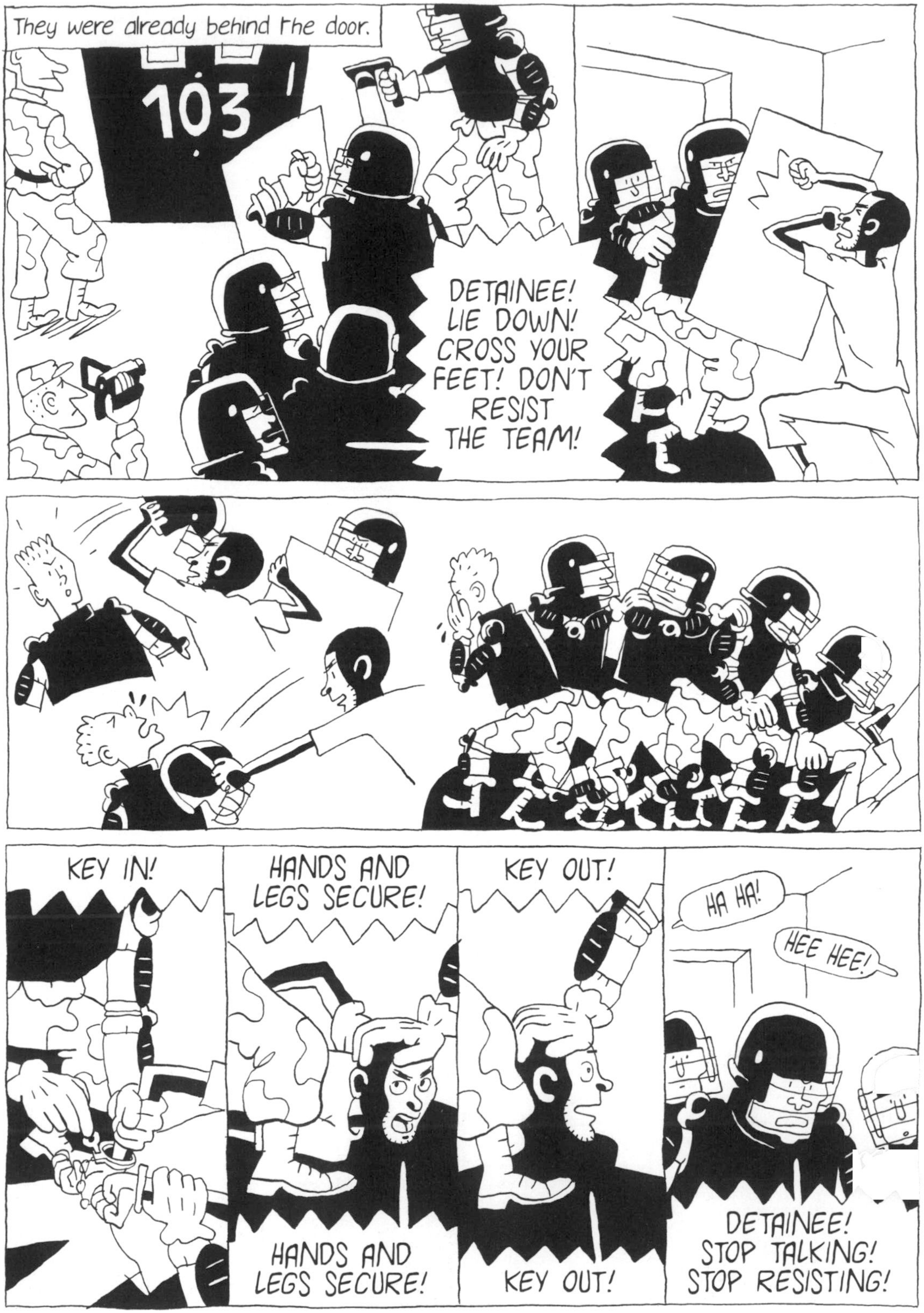
They were already behind the door.
103
DETAINEE! LIE DOWN! CROSS YOUR FEET! DON'T RESIST THE TEAM!
KEY IN!
HANDS AND LEGS SECURE!
HANDS AND LEGS SECURE!
KEY OUT!
KEY OUT!
HA HA!
HEE HEE!
DETAINEE! STOP TALKING! STOP RESISTING!

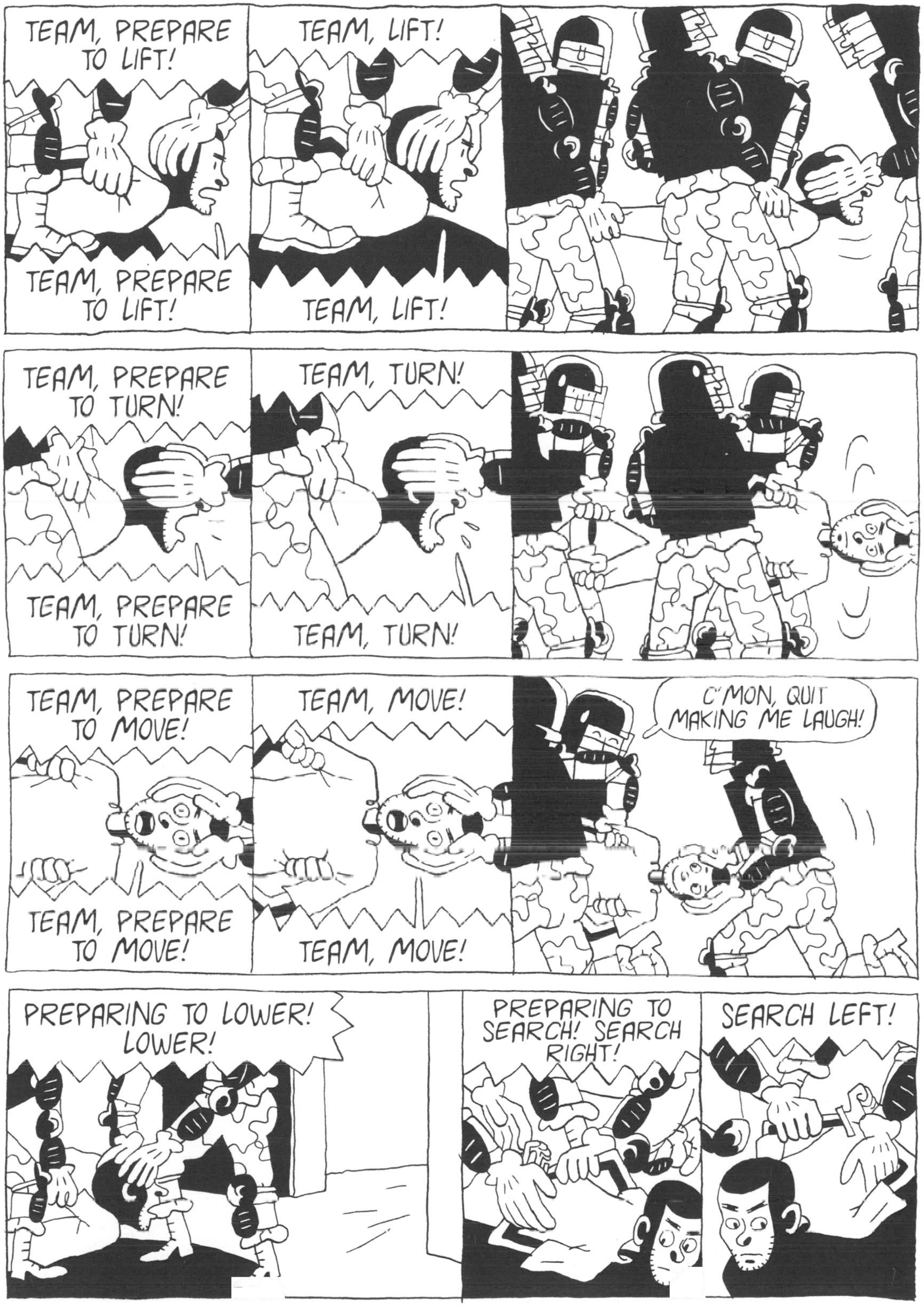
TEAM, PREPARE TO LIFT!
TEAM, PREPARE TO LIFT!
TEAM, LIFT!
TEAM, LIFT!
TEAM, PREPARE TO TURN!
TEAM, PREPARE TO TURN!
TEAM, TURN!
TEAM, TURN!
TEAM, PREPARE TO MOVE!
TEAM, PREPARE TO MOVE!
TEAM, MOVE!
TEAM, MOVE!
C'MON, QUIT MAKING ME LAUGH!
PREPARING TO LOWER! LOWER!
PREPARING TO SEARCH! SEARCH RIGHT!
SEARCH LEFT!

CELL IS CLEAR! SEND HIM BACK!

Later that night, the colonel came to the block. He noticed it was really cold.

In the morning:

BROTHERS, I'M HERE TO FIX THE A.C.!

HOORAY!

106 105 103

THANKS!

NONE TOO SOON!

Everybody was happy. And we were finally able to go to sleep.

ZZZZZ... ZZZZZ...

Two weeks later.

CHRIS TUCKER, LAWYER VISIT!

CLIVE STAFFORD SMITH, director of Reprieve, a legal action charity representing many detainees.

ALL YOUR BROTHERS IN THE CAMP FOUND OUT ABOUT WHAT YOU DID, AND THANK YOU.

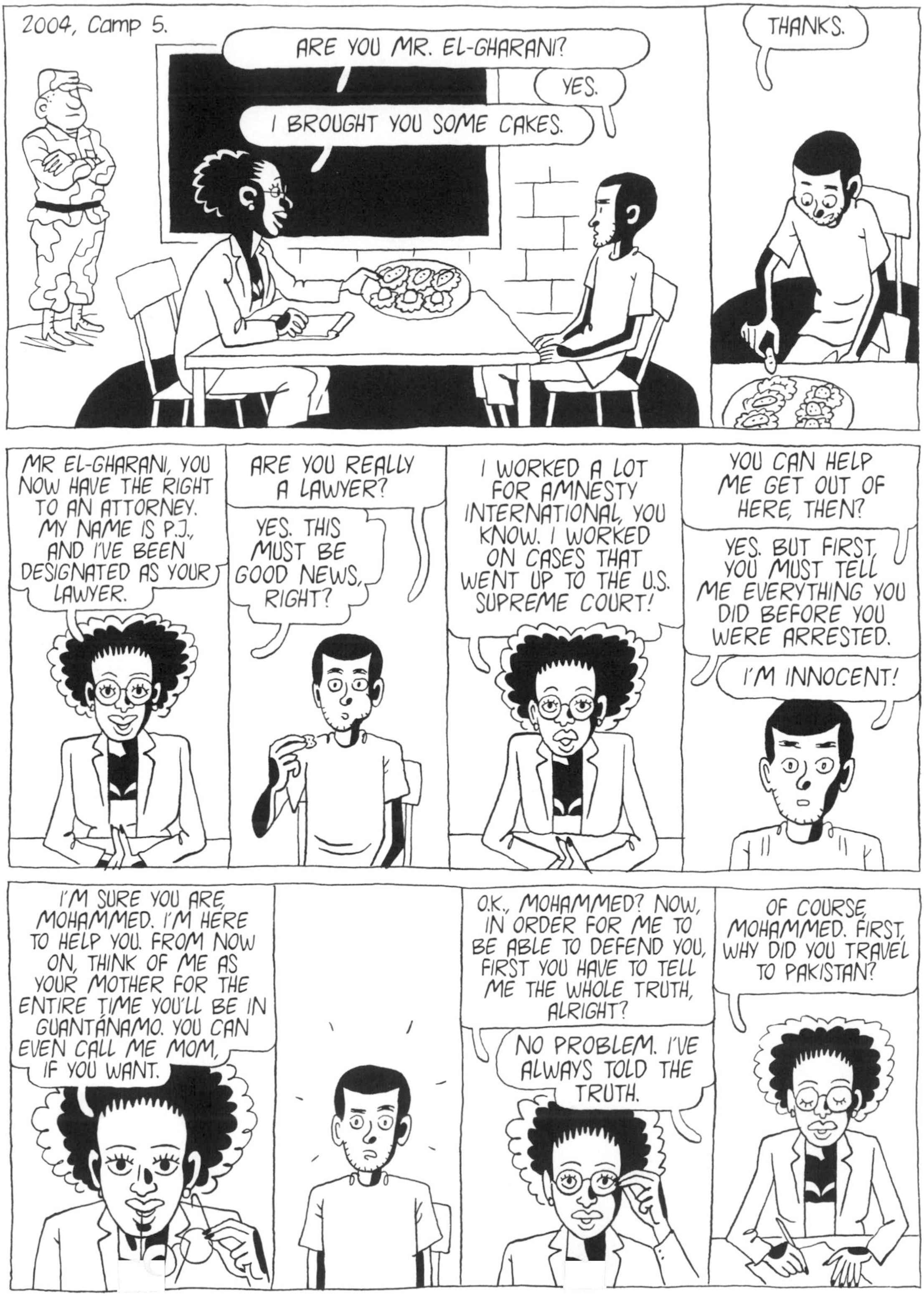
2004, Camp 5.
ARE YOU MR. EL-GHARANI?
YES.
I BROUGHT YOU SOME CAKES.
THANKS.
MR EL-GHARANI, YOU NOW HAVE THE RIGHT TO AN ATTORNEY. MY NAME IS P.J., AND I'VE BEEN DESIGNATED AS YOUR LAWYER.
ARE YOU REALLY A LAWYER?
YES. THIS MUST BE GOOD NEWS, RIGHT?
I WORKED A LOT FOR AMNESTY INTERNATIONAL, YOU KNOW. I WORKED ON CASES THAT WENT UP TO THE U.S. SUPREME COURT!
YOU CAN HELP ME GET OUT OF HERE, THEN?
YES. BUT FIRST, YOU MUST TELL ME EVERYTHING YOU DID BEFORE YOU WERE ARRESTED.
I'M INNOCENT!
I'M SURE YOU ARE, MOHAMMED. I'M HERE TO HELP YOU. FROM NOW ON, THINK OF ME AS YOUR MOTHER FOR THE ENTIRE TIME YOU'LL BE IN GUANTÁNAMO. YOU CAN EVEN CALL ME MOM, IF YOU WANT.
O.K., MOHAMMED? NOW, IN ORDER FOR ME TO BE ABLE TO DEFEND YOU, FIRST YOU HAVE TO TELL ME THE WHOLE TRUTH, ALRIGHT?
NO PROBLEM. I'VE ALWAYS TOLD THE TRUTH.
OF COURSE, MOHAMMED. FIRST, WHY DID YOU TRAVEL TO PAKISTAN?

Later.

YES, HE'S THE ONE I HAVE TO INTERROGATE...

....

HEY, YOU! WHAT THE FUCK ARE YOU DOING IN THE BLOCK?

A 213

YOU CAME TO INTERROGATE A BROTHER? YOU'RE NOT A LAWYER?

NO, I'M AN INTERROGATOR.

YOU LIED TO ME!

269, I'M ONLY DOING MY JOB. AND MY JOB IS TO GET THE TRUTH.

LYING TO GET THE TRUTH? THAT'S YOUR JOB?! I'M NOT SAYING ANOTHER WORD TO YOU!

Before 2004, there were no lawyers in Guantánamo. When we asked for a lawyer, the guards would just laugh. I think Clive was the first lawyer in Guantánamo.

To start with, he defended Shaker Aamer. Then Shaker told him about me.

YOU SHOULD DEFEND HIM TOO. HE'S THE YOUNGEST PRISONER HERE. HE WAS 13 WHEN HE WAS ARRESTED.

REALLY?

YES, BUT THE AMERICANS ALWAYS TREATED HIM LIKE AN ADULT. PLUS, YOU WON'T NEED AN INTERPRETER, HE ALREADY SPEAKS GOOD ENGLISH. HE'S A GOOD BOY.

WHAT'S HIS NAME?

EL-GHARANI.

I MEAN, WHAT'S HIS NUMBER?

269.

At first, I didn't trust Clive.

MY NAME IS CLIVE STAFFORD SMITH. I AM YOUR FRIEND SHAKER'S LAWYER. HE WAS THE ONE WHO ASKED ME TO HELP YOU.

WE'RE NOT ALLOWED TO HAVE LAWYERS HERE.

NOW YOU HAVE A RIGHT TO. WE FOUGHT FOR IT.

ONCE BEFORE, A WOMAN CAME AND TOLD ME SHE WAS A LAWYER. LATER, I REALIZED SHE WAS AN INTERROGATOR. WHO'S TO SAY YOU'RE NOT LYING TOO?

I'M NOT LYING. HERE ARE MY PASSPORT, MY I.D. CARD, AND OTHER PAPERS PROVING THAT I'M A LAWYER. LOOK THEM OVER. TAKE YOUR TIME.

BEFORE YOU CAME, SOME GUARDS TOLD ME TO BEWARE, THAT YOU WERE AN ENEMY OF ISLAM.

THEY TOLD OTHER CLIENTS OF MINE THE SAME THING. THEY'RE THE ONES LYING TO YOU.

WHY DID YOU PICK ME?

BECAUSE YOU'RE THE YOUNGEST. THAT'S WHAT SHAKER TOLD ME.

THIS IS THE PHONE NUMBER OF MY FAMILY IN SAUDI ARABIA. CAN YOU CALL THEM? TELL THEM I'M ALIVE, TELL THEM I'M HERE.

Before the lawyers were allowed in, we didn't know what was going on outside. And outside, our families didn't know how we were doing. We weren't allowed to write letters or call our families.

Later.

MOHAMMED, I SPOKE TO YOUR FAMILY. THEY WERE GLAD TO GET NEWS ABOUT YOU. THEY'RE HAPPY TO KNOW YOU'RE ALIVE AND HOPE YOU'LL GET RELEASED SOON.

THANK YOU!

YOUR FAMILY ALSO SENT US YOUR BIRTH CERTIFICATE. IT WASN'T THAT DIFFICULT. IT'S UNBELIEVABLE THAT THE AMERICANS NEVER REQUESTED IT.

NO, IT'S NOT SURPRISING. SINCE I'VE BEEN HERE, I'VE LEARNED SOMETHING — THE AMERICANS ARE NOT TRYING TO FIND OUT THE TRUTH.

AT ANY RATE, IT PROVES YOU WERE A MINOR WHEN YOU WERE ARRESTED. THEY WON'T BE ABLE TO DENY IT ANYMORE. THEY HAD NO RIGHT TO TREAT YOU AS AN ADULT WHEN YOU WERE A JUVENILE.

UNDER U.S. LAW AND INTERNATIONAL LAW, EVERYONE UNDER 18 IS A "JUVENILE" AND SHOULD BE TREATED AS SUCH.

I WOULD SAY DESPITE THEIR AGE, THESE ARE VERY, VERY DANGEROUS PEOPLE... THEY MAY BE "JUVENILES", BUT THEY'RE NOT ON A LITTLE LEAGUE TEAM ANYWHERE. THEY'RE ON A MAJOR LEAGUE TEAM, AND IT'S A TERRORIST TEAM. AND THEY'RE IN GUANTÁNAMO FOR VERY GOOD REASON: FOR OUR SAFETY, FOR YOUR SAFETY.

WE DON'T PLAN ON, ER, DETAINING, ER... "JUVENILES" AT GUANTÁNAMO FURTHER. ER... I CAN'T SAY IN TERMS OF THE FUTURE OF ANYWHERE ELSE...

Major General Geoffrey D. Miller, Commander, Joint Task Force at Guantánamo, 2003

Lieutenant Commander Barbara Burfeind, Department of Defense spokesperson, 2004

MOHAMMED, WE'RE GOING TO COURT, AGAINST THE U.S. GOVERNMENT. WE'LL NEED THE MEDIA FOR THAT. WE HAVE TO TELL THE MEDIA WHAT'S GOING ON HERE, HOW YOU'RE BEING TREATED.

LOOK. THEY TORTURE US.

WE'LL HAVE TO SAY THAT THERE ARE PRISONERS HERE WHO WERE MINORS WHEN THEY WERE ARRESTED...

THERE WAS ONE GUY AS YOUNG AS I WAS, MOHAMMED JAWAD, FROM AFGHANISTAN.

Clive was right. People outside started to find out the story of those of us in Guantánamo.

This guy was a teacher in Pakistan, that one was a doctor in Pakistan: were they really with al-Qaida?

The interrogators began to worry. In February 2007:

269, SOME ADVICE: BETTER NOT TO TALK TO YOUR LAWYER ABOUT THE F.B.I. AGENTS WHO INTERROGATED YOU IN 2003.

MOHAMMED, THIS MAN IS A REAL F.B.I. AGENT. HE WOULD LIKE TO KNOW IF F.B.I. AGENTS RESORTED TO ILLEGAL INTERROGATION TECHNIQUES.

OR IF SOME INTERROGATORS FROM OTHER AGENCIES PRETENDED TO BE F.B.I. AGENTS...

FEDERAL FBI BUREAU OF INVESTIGATION

CAN YOU DESCRIBE THE PEOPLE WHO INTERROGATED YOU FOR ME? WHAT THEY LOOKED LIKE, THE QUESTIONS THEY ASKED YOU?

Later.

CHRIS, TRANSFER!

YOU'RE ALONE IN THIS BLOCK. NO ONE TO CHAT WITH.

YOU WERE WARNED — YOU TALK TOO MUCH!

Later.

269!

The Team

cameraman

medic

Egyptian interpreter

2 officers

103

WASSUP, MEN, WE GOT MEDIA HERE?

269, WE KNOW YOU HAVE A NEEDLE ON YOU. ONE GUARD SAW YOUR LAWYER GIVE IT TO YOU. WE WANT TO SEE YOU NAKED.

NO PROBLEM.

NO FIGHT?

WANT MY UNDERWEAR TOO? O.K.

They took my clothes for searching and gave me new ones.

The Egyptian interpreter:

عَملتَ كويس، كانوا راح يربحوا عليك

[YOU DID A GOOD JOB, THEY WERE GOING TO BEAT YOU UP.]

2008

GOOD NEWS, MOHAMMED! YOU'RE GETTING A TRIAL. UNFORTUNATELY, THE JUDGE ISN'T REALLY THE NICEST GUY. UNTIL NOW, HE'S ALWAYS BEEN ON THE GOVERNMENT SIDE — THREE DETAINEES WHO APPEARED BEFORE HIM LOST. BUT... FINGERS CROSSED!

ZACHARY KATZNELSON, LAWYER WORKING WITH CLIVE STAFFORD SMITH

THE TRIAL TOOK PLACE IN D.C. WITH ME STILL IN GUANTÁNAMO. WE LISTENED TO THE DEBATES THROUGH A BIG PHONE WITH SPEAKERS. I COULDN'T TALK. I COULD ONLY LISTEN.

17 December 2008.

Government counsel: THE FILE INDICATES THAT THE PETITIONER WAS A MEMBER OF AN AL-QAIDA CELL IN LONDON, LED BY ABU QATADA AL-MASRI. THE SOURCE OF THIS INFORMATION IS ANOTHER MEMBER OF THIS CELL. THIS WAS IN 1993.

Mohammed's counsel: YOUR HONOR, THAT'S ABSOLUTE NONSENSE! IN 1993, MY CLIENT WAS NO MORE THAN 6! AND HE'D SIMPLY NEVER SET FOOT IN LONDON!

Judge: THE COURT HAS HEARD BOTH PARTIES. THE DECISION WILL BE ANNOUNCED IN TWO WEEKS.

Almost a month later, I still had no news. At the time, I was still in Segregation.

14 January 2009.

HEY, 269, YOU'VE GOT AN APPOINTMENT!

WHERE?

PHONE CALL FOR YOU. YOU COMING OR NOT?

That afternoon, I was given a white uniform instead of the orange one I'd worn most of the time since my arrival. White was the color for those cleared for release.

**UNITED STATES DISTRICT COURT
FOR THE DISTRICT OF COLUMBIA**

MOHAMMED EL GHARANI,   )
    Petitioner,   )
)   Civil Case No. 05-429 (RJL)
    v.   )
)
GEORGE W. BUSH, *et al.*,   )
    Respondents.   )

MEMORANDUM ORDER
(January _14_, 2009)

Petitioner Mohammed el Gharani ("petitioner" or "el Gharani") is a detainee being held at the U.S. Naval Base at Guantanamo Bay, Cuba. He alleges that he is being unlawfully detained by Respondents President George W. Bush, Secretary of Defense Robert M. Gates,[1] Army Brigade General Jay Hood, and Army Colonel Nelson J. Cannon (collectively "respondents" or the "Government"). On December 17, 2008, the Court commenced habeas corpus hearings for petitioner el Gharani. That morning, counsel for both parties made unclassified opening statements in a public hearing. Petitioner el Gharani listened to the opening statements via a live telephone transmission to Guantanamo Bay, Cuba.

Judge RICHARD J. LEON

UNLIKE MOST OF THE OTHER CASES REVIEWED TO DATE BY THIS COURT, THE GOVERNMENT'S EVIDENCE AGAINST EL-GHARANI CONSISTS PRINCIPALLY OF THE STATEMENTS MADE BY TWO OTHER DETAINEES WHILE INCARCERATED AT GUANTÁNAMO BAY... THE CREDIBILITY AND RELIABILITY OF THE DETAINEES BEING RELIED UPON BY THE GOVERNMENT HAS... BEEN DIRECTLY CALLED INTO QUESTION BY GOVERNMENT PERSONNEL.

PUTTING ASIDE THE OBVIOUS AND UNANSWERED QUESTIONS AS TO HOW A SAUDI MINOR FROM A VERY POOR FAMILY COULD HAVE EVEN BECOME A MEMBER OF A LONDON-BASED CELL, THE GOVERNMENT SIMPLY ADVANCES NO CORROBORATING EVIDENCE FOR THESE STATEMENTS IT BELIEVES TO BE RELIABLE FROM A FELLOW DETAINEE, THE BASIS OF WHOSE KNOWLEDGE IS — AT BEST — UNKNOWN.

SIMPLY STATED, A MOSAIC OF TILES BEARING IMAGES THIS MURKY REVEALS NOTHING ABOUT THE PETITIONER WITH SUFFICIENT CLARITY...

IT IS HEREBY ORDERED...

THAT RESPONDENTS ARE DIRECTED TO TAKE ALL NECESSARY AND APPROPRIATE DIPLOMATIC STEPS TO FACILITATE THE RELEASE OF PETITIONER EL-GHARANI FORTHWITH.

CONCLUSION

For all the foregoing reasons, and for the reasons in the forthcoming classified version of this opinion, it is hereby

ORDERED that petitioner Mohammed el Gharani's petition for writ of habeas corpus is **GRANTED**. It is further

ORDERED that respondents are directed to take all necessary and appropriate diplomatic steps to facilitate the release of petitioner el Gharani forthwith.

SO ORDERED.

RICHARD J. LEON
United States District Judge

ZACHARY KATZNELSON:

IT'S A FANTASTIC RESULT!

JUDGE LEON DID JUSTICE TODAY. THIS IS AN INNOCENT KID, ONLY 14 YEARS OLD, WHO WAS SEIZED ILLEGALLY BY THE PAKISTANIS. HE NEVER SHOULD HAVE BEEN SEIZED IN THE FIRST PLACE. HE'S SPENT ONE-THIRD OF HIS LIFE IN GUANTÁNAMO...

UNITED STATES COURT HOUSE

WE MIGHT GET A BLACK PRESIDENT! IF HE'S ELECTED, THINGS WILL BE BETTER FOR YOU GUYS. HE'LL CLEAN UP ALL THE SHIT HERE.

YOU THINK HE CAN WIN?

I REALLY HOPE SO FOR YOU GUYS.

HOPE

HIS NAME'S OBAMA. HE PROMISED TO SHUT DOWN GUANTÁNAMO. HE ASKED FOR DETAINEES TO BE WELL TREATED IN THE MEANTIME. GUANTÁNAMO HAS BECOME A NIGHTMARE FOR THE U.S.

4 NOVEMBER

On 4 November 2008, Barack Obama was elected President of the United States. All the brothers must have been happy, but I couldn't enjoy it, as I was still in segregation in Echo Block.

14 JANUARY

On 14 January 2009, Judge Leon ordered my release.

20 JANUARY

On 20 January, Barack Obama took office. And on 22 January:

THIS FIRST EXECUTIVE ORDER THAT WE ARE SIGNING: BY THE AUTHORITY VESTED IN ME AS PRESIDENT BY THE CONSTITUTION UNDER THE LAWS OF THE UNITED STATES OF AMERICA...

...IN ORDER TO EFFECT THE APPROPRIATE DISPOSITION OF INDIVIDUALS CURRENTLY DETAINED BY THE DEPARTMENT OF DEFENSE AT GUANTÁNAMO, AND PROMPTLY TO CLOSE THE DETENTION FACILITY AT GUANTÁNAMO, CONSISTENT WITH THE NATIONAL SECURITY AND FOREIGN POLICY INTERESTS OF THE UNITED STATES AND THE INTEREST OF JUSTICE, I HEREBY ORDER...

AND WE THEN PROVIDE THE PROCESS WHEREBY GUANTÁNAMO WILL BE CLOSED NO LATER THAN ONE YEAR FROM NOW. WE WILL BE—

IS THERE A SEPARATE EXECUTIVE ORDER, GREG, WITH RESPECT TO HOW WE'RE GOING TO DISPOSE OF THE DETAINEES?

WE WILL SET UP A PROCESS.

WE WILL BE SETTING UP A PROCESS WHEREBY THIS IS GOING TO BE TAKING PLACE.

THE INDIVIDUALS WHO ARE STANDING BEHIND ME... ARE OUTSTANDING AMERICANS WHO HAVE FOUGHT FOR AND DEFENDED THIS COUNTRY. AND FOR THEM TO FIGHT ON BEHALF OF OUR CONSTITUTIONAL IDEALS AND VALUES, I THINK, IS EXCEPTIONAL...

SO I WANTED TO MAKE SURE THAT THEY WERE HERE TO WITNESS THE SIGNING OF THIS EXECUTIVE ORDER.

THERE WE GO!

CLAP
CLAP
CLAP

CLAP
CLAP
CLAP

One month after my trial, they moved me to Camp Iguana.

Originally, Iguana was for the juvenile prisoners. But since I had been treated as an adult, I had never been there. Now, Iguana was used as a transit camp for those who had been found innocent and were awaiting release, which could take months. Before they moved me to Iguana, they had warned everyone there, brothers and guards alike: "El-Gharani's coming. Watch out! He'll make trouble, break the cameras, etc."

It was true, Iguana was a better camp, more open. There were only twenty detainees, mostly Uighurs.* We were four to a cell. The doors were open, and we could visit brothers in the other cells.

For the first time in seven years, I had a pillow and a real blanket. We also had a fridge, a microwave, and books. I was reading Agatha Christie's stories. I also liked Roots,** about African-American history.

In the other camps, they shackled or cuffed our hands and feet to shower, but not in Iguana. And here you could go to shower any time you wanted! We had the option to wear civilian clothes. We could see the sea, breathe fresh air, touch the sand. I even saw the iguanas, they'd come up just outside the camp.

*In 2001, 22 members of the Uighur Muslim Chinese minority were arrested in Pakistan and, like Mohammed, sold for $5,000 each to the U.S. authorities. They remained in Iguana until various countries agreed to take them. Six of them were sent to the Palau Islands in the Pacific Ocean.
** In Roots, novelist Alex Haley told the story of his family since being brought as slaves to the U.S.

Even in Iguana, they still did lots of stupid things. For instance, curfew was at 9 p.m., and we each had to go back to our cells. As soon as I heard that:

The next day, everyone began to defy the curfew.

Some assholes would give us tiny helpings of food and throw out the leftovers.

We were also able to change lots of stuff there. Often our problems were with the guards. Some were bullying us just for fun. After seven years, I knew the system. And I knew that if you make trouble, the "big dogs" come and can make things better.

In Iguana, we were allowed one phone call to our family every two weeks. An Egyptian interpreter listened in, and could cut it short at any time, for no reason.

The Americans had contacted the Saudi Red Crescent, who had called my family to an office in Riyadh, one hour from Medina by plane. I had not spoken to my parents for seven years. We were all very moved.

Life was better for me, but in the other camps, my brothers were still suffering. Three nights in a row, the smell of pepper spray came from Camp Echo.

We decided to do this on a Sunday, when the "big dogs" weren't working. LAKHDAR was on watch. I covered the living room's camera...

I had the number of Sami al-Hajj, a former detainee working for Al Jazeera.* He'd been among those who taught me English.

* Al Jazeera cameraman Sami al-Hajj was arrested and held at Guantánamo for six years for questioning about the television network's "training program, telecommunications equipment, and newsgathering operations in Chechnya, Kosovo, and Afghanistan", including contacts with terrorist groups. When he was released, in 2008, he resumed working for Al Jazeera in Qatar.

21-YEAR-OLD MOHAMMED EL-GHARANI HAS BEEN HELD IN GUANTÁNAMO FOR SIX YEARS. HE'S DUE TO BE RELEASED SOON. BUT FROM THE HOLDING CAMP IN GUANTÁNAMO PRISON WHERE HE'S WAITING TO BE FREED, HE PHONED AL JAZEERA'S SAMI AL-HAJJ, HIMSELF A FORMER GUANTÁNAMO DETAINEE.

... I MEAN, MY BROTHER, I REFUSED TO LEAVE MY CELL. THEY WERE NOT GRANTING ME MY RIGHTS! I WAS ONLY DEMANDING MY BASIC RIGHTS LIKE EXERCISE, MEETING OTHER INMATES, AND EATING NORMAL FOOD...

SO A GROUP OF SIX SOLDIERS WEARING PROTECTIVE GEAR AND HELMETS CAME TO MY CELL. THEY WERE ACCOMPANIED BY A SOLDIER CARRYING A CAMERA AND ONE WITH TEAR GAS. THEY HAD A THICK RUBBER OR PLASTIC BATON. THEY BEAT ME WITH IT.

THEY EMPTIED OUT ABOUT TWO CANISTERS OF TEAR GAS ON ME. AFTER, I STOPPED TALKING, AND TEARS WERE FLOWING FROM MY EYES, I COULD HARDLY SEE OR BREATHE. THEY THEN BEAT ME AGAIN TO THE GROUND. ONE OF THEM HELD MY HEAD AND BEAT IT AGAINST THE GROUND. I STARTED SCREAMING TO A SENIOR: "SEE WHAT HE'S DOING! SEE WHAT HE'S DOING!" THE SENIOR STARTED LAUGHING AND SAID: "HE'S DOING HIS JOB." HE BROKE ONE OF MY TEETH. OF COURSE, THEY DIDN'T FILM THE BLOOD. THEY FILMED MY BACK SO IT DOESN'T SHOW.

THE CHADIAN CITIZEN WAS 15 YEARS OLD WHEN CAPTURED IN PAKISTAN. HE WAS ACCUSED OF BEING A MEMBER OF AL-QAIDA AND TRANSFERRED TO GUANTÁNAMO. A U.S. FEDERAL JUDGE ORDERED EL-GHARANI'S RELEASE THREE MONTHS AGO, ARGUING THAT THERE WAS NO EVIDENCE TO JUSTIFY HIS DETENTION. HE HAS BEEN IN A PROVISIONAL FACILITY SINCE THEN, WHERE INMATES ARE ALLOWED TO CONTACT THEIR FAMILIES BY PHONE. HE SAYS THE DETAINEES' TREATMENT HAS NOT CHANGED SINCE PRESIDENT OBAMA TOOK OFFICE AND ORDERED THE CLOSURE OF THE PRISON BY THE END OF 2009.

MOHAMMED, HAVE THINGS CHANGED SINCE OBAMA BECAME PRESIDENT?

NO, THERE'S STILL BAD TREATMENT. YOU REMEMBER ███████, THE YEMENI? THEY BROKE HIS TEETH. IT'S STILL THE SAME.

THIS TREATMENT STARTED ABOUT TWENTY DAYS BEFORE OBAMA CAME INTO POWER, AND SINCE THEN, I'VE BEEN SUBJECTED TO THE SAME TREATMENT ALMOST EVERY DAY. SINCE OBAMA TOOK CHARGE, HE HAS NOT SHOWN US THAT ANYTHING WILL CHANGE.

AL JAZEERA PROVIDED DETAILED INFORMATION OF THE PHONE CALL TO THE PENTAGON AND THE DEPARTMENT OF JUSTICE, AND ONLY RECEIVED A REPLY FROM THE SPOKESMAN OF GUANTÁNAMO PRISON:

YOU MEAN, FROM WHAT I UNDERSTAND OF YOUR RESPONSE, THAT THIS IS NOT TRUE?

BROOK DEWALT
GUANTÁNAMO PRISON SPOKESMAN

I HAVE NO RECORD OF THE AUTHENTICITY OF THIS, ER, IT'S AN ALLEGED PHONE TRANSCRIPT AND, ER, AND SO, ER, IT'S ALLEGED, WE DON'T HAVE ANY EVIDENCE SUPPORTING OR SUBSTANTIATING, ER, ANY OF THESE CLAIMS.

THE OBAMA ADMINISTRATION HAS CONDEMNED THE TREATMENT OF GUANTÁNAMO PRISONERS, BUT THE NUMBER OF REPORTS OF ABUSE HAS INCREASED IN THE LAST MONTH, ACCORDING TO CIVIL RIGHTS LAWYERS.

AHMED GHAPPOUR
REPRIEVE GROUP

I FILED AT LEAST THREE SETS OF COMPLAINTS SINCE DECEMBER 22ND, WITH THE MILITARY, AND EACH ONE OF THOSE COMPLAINTS CALLED FOR AN INVESTIGATION, SPECIFIED GUARDS BY NUMBER, SPECIFIED INCIDENTS BY DATE. AND I HAVE NOT HEARD BACK FROM A SINGLE ONE OF THESE COMPLAINTS THAT I FILED.

THERE ARE STILL MORE THAN 240 PRISONERS IN GUANTÁNAMO. THEIR CASES ARE BEING REVIEWED BY THE U.S. JUSTICE DEPARTMENT. BUT FOR NOW, THEIR SITUATION, AND THEIR FUTURE TREATMENT, REMAIN UNCERTAIN... MONICA VILLAMIZAR, AL JAZEERA, WASHINGTON.

I didn't know what he was talking about. It had been two weeks since I had called Sami al-Hajj.

SOONER OR LATER, I'M GOING TO GET OUT, AND PEOPLE WILL KNOW. I'LL DO MY BEST TO TELL THE WHOLE WORLD.

YOU DID ALL THIS, AND FOR WHAT? BEFORE GUANTÁNAMO, YOU DIDN'T KNOW ME, AND I DIDN'T KNOW YOU...

YOU'RE THE BOSS, THE ONE WHO GIVES THE ORDERS, CALLS IN THE TEAM. DON'T THINK PEOPLE ARE GOING TO FORGET THIS...

WHO'S A CRIMINAL? YOU'RE THE CRIMINAL!

THAT'S ENOUGH.

NO, IT'S NOT! BUT SEVEN YEARS IS ENOUGH!

O.K., 269, YOU GOT ME. YOU'RE RIGHT.

After that, as a punishment, they moved me to Camp Delta. At the time, it was empty. I was the only one there, alone in a block. It lasted three weeks.

grey uniform

4 guards, changing every 12 hours.

Later.

YOUR BROTHERS SAY "SALAAM" AND THANK YOU FOR WHAT YOU DID. THEY WANT TO TELL YOU THAT YOU'VE BEEN BRAVE, BUT NOW YOU SHOULD STOP.

I hoped to go back to Medina.

I'M SORRY, MOHAMMED, BUT I DON'T THINK THAT WILL BE POSSIBLE.

SAUDI ARABIA DOESN'T CONSIDER YOU A CITIZEN, AND DOESN'T WANT YOU BACK. YOU'LL HAVE TO GO TO CHAD, IF THEY AGREE TO TAKE YOU. OR SOMEWHERE ELSE...

CHAD! WHAT WILL I DO THERE?

I DON'T KNOW ANYBODY IN CHAD, I DON'T KNOW THE COUNTRY.

IT COULD BE WORSE. THINK OF THE UIGHURS — THEY CAN'T GO BACK TO CHINA AND HAVE BEEN SENT TO AN ISLAND IN THE MIDDLE OF THE PACIFIC OCEAN!

At first, the Chadians wouldn't take me. Then they changed their minds.

MAHMOUD ADAM BÉCHIR,
Chadian ambassador to the U.S.

AS WE SEE IT, EL-GHARANI IS AN INNOCENT CHADIAN CITIZEN UNFAIRLY IMPRISONED. I PROMISE THAT WE WILL DO EVERYTHING TO WELCOME HIM TO CHAD, HIS COUNTRY. WE WILL HELP HIM, WE WILL GIVE HIM A HOUSE AND A JOB. HE WILL BE WELL TREATED. THE PRESIDENT HIMSELF WILL GREET HIM!

Excerpts from a cable from the U.S. Embassy in N'Djamena, dated 9 November 2007, leaked by WikiLeaks.

SUBJECT: CHAD: FOREIGN MINISTRY RESPONDS ON GUANTANAMO CASE

REF: A. SECSTATE 70395   ¶B. NDJAMENA 445   ¶1.

(SBU) Summary: President Deby has directed his Ministry of Foreign Affairs to take steps to seek the liberation of Chadian Guantanamo detainee Mohamed Algharani (aka Yousef Abkir Salih Al Qarani).

(...)   Note: President Deby's decision to seek Algharani's release appears to have been prompted by the visit of members of the UK-based "Reprieve" organization who met with high ranking Chadian officials on the case.

(...)   An internal report prepared for President Deby on the meeting between Zakary Katz Nelson, Legislative Director of Reprieve (identified in the report as an American lawyer) and the Deputy Director of the President's Civil Cabinet, Mahamat Saleh Adoum.

(...)   Adoum notes that "our country cannot avoid its obligations towards citizens under arbitrary detention abroad...the continued detention of a compatriot for motives decidedly lacking in glory is assuredly a major handicap in our continued efforts to improve our country's image in the world." He suggests that "the President order the government to undertake the necessary demarches to obtain his repatriation."   -- The handwritten response of President Deby on the note states: "Undertake demarches to obtain his liberation."

June 2009.

WHAT SIZE DO YOU WEAR?

L OR XL.

When I arrived at Guantánamo, my size was "Small".

They were always releasing detainees at night time. They brought me blue trousers, a white T-shirt, and a denim jacket.

MAY I SHAKE HANDS WITH MY BROTHERS?

NO WAY.

It was the custom, for detainees who were released, to walk up and down their block twice to say goodbye to the brothers. But in Mike Block, I was alone.

CAN I AT LEAST SAY GOODBYE TO SHAKER?

NO.

Shaker was in P Block, just on the other side of the road between Delta 2 and Delta 3. When I was walked near his block:

UNCLE SHAKER, I'M LEAVING! I'M GOING HOME!

!

GOOD LUCK, SUNBUL! I WISH YOU THE BEST, MY BROTHER, MAY GOD BE WITH YOU!

They took me to a big bus. I recognized a guy sitting up front, an Iraqi in his 40s. We called him Abu Fatima. He was also being released. We were happy.

We felt the bus drive onto a boat. After thirty minutes, we docked and drove to the airport. I saw the biggest plane I had ever seen in my life. About a hundred guards were surrounding the place. What were they thinking? That maybe I was going to hijack the plane and attack the U.S.?

44132

NO TALKING, NO MOVING!

In the plane, they searched us and covered our eyes and ears.

I couldn't sleep. I kept thinking about what was going to happen. It was a long flight, the longest of my life. My handcuffs were too tight. One of my ears was hurting.

After that, we could see the guards all around. I counted more than fifty.

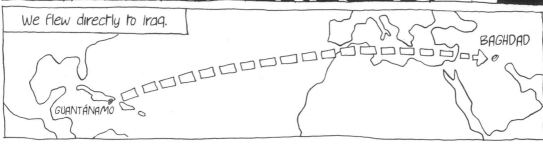

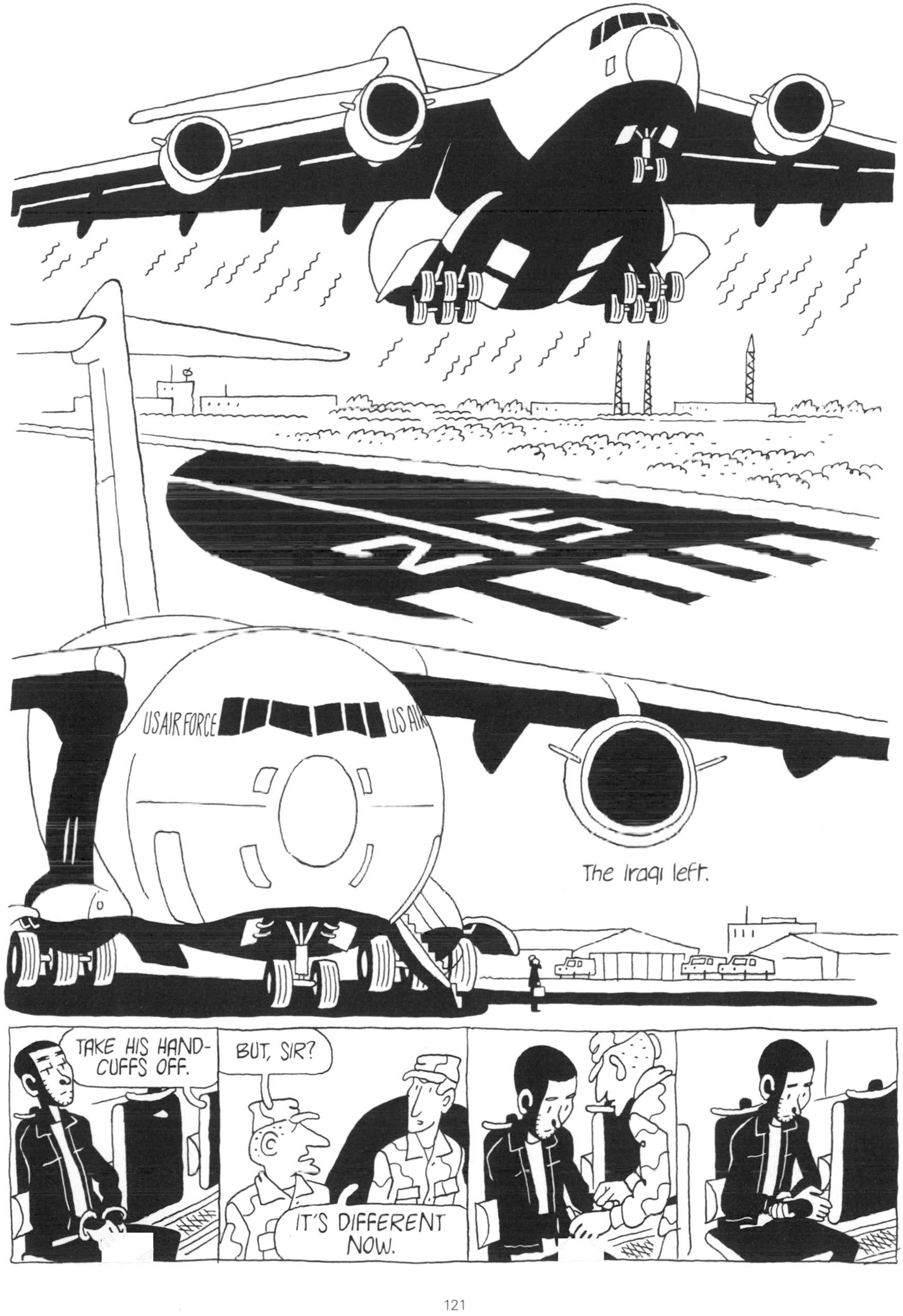

US AIR FORCE
US AIR
The Iraqi left.
TAKE HIS HAND-CUFFS OFF.
BUT, SIR?
IT'S DIFFERENT NOW.

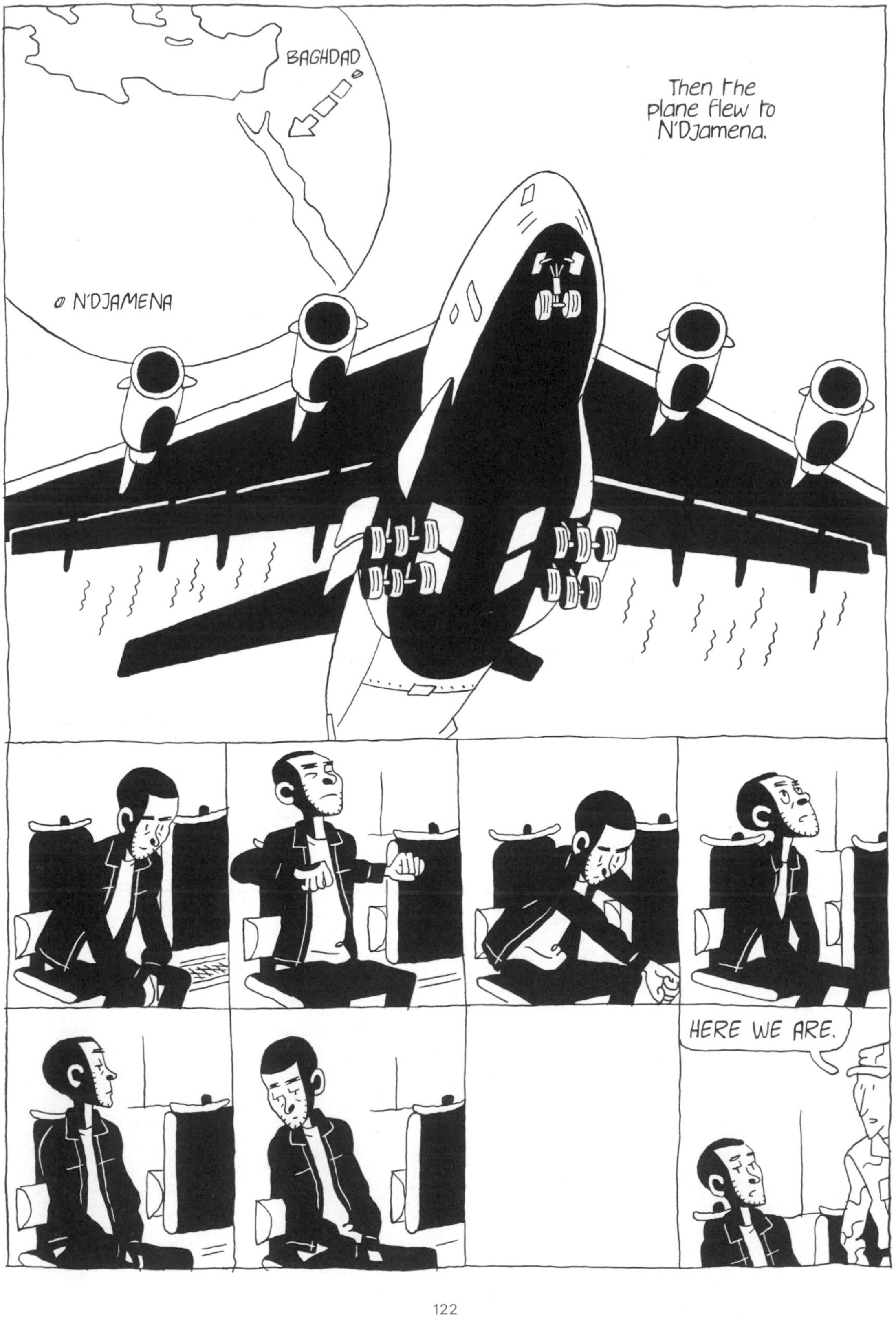
BAGHDAD
Then the plane flew to N'Djamena.
N'DJAMENA
HERE WE ARE.

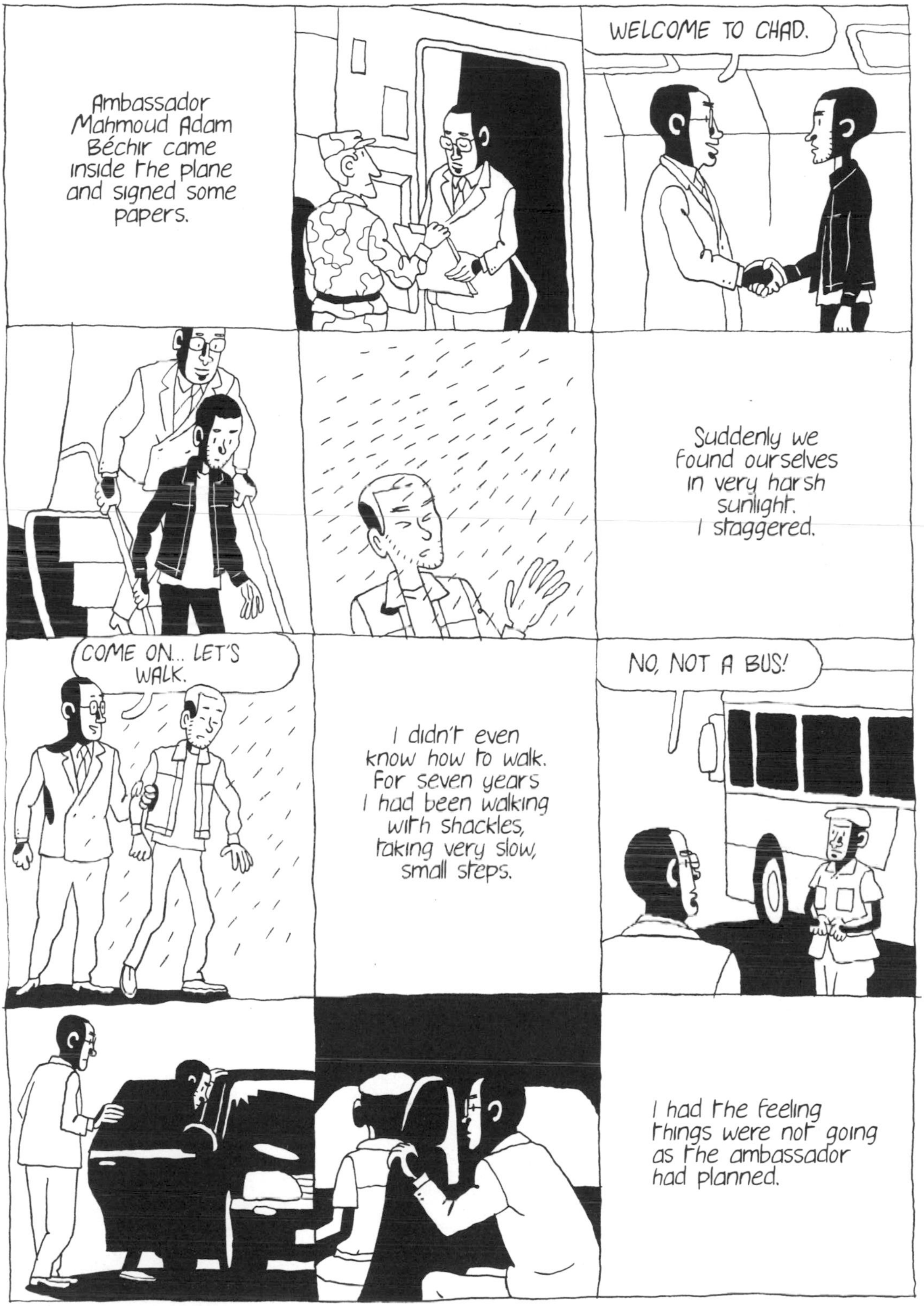
Ambassador Mahmoud Adam Béchir came inside the plane and signed some papers.
WELCOME TO CHAD.
Suddenly we found ourselves in very harsh sunlight. I staggered.
COME ON... LET'S WALK.
I didn't even know how to walk. For seven years I had been walking with shackles, taking very slow, small steps.
NO, NOT A BUS!
I had the feeling things were not going as the ambassador had planned.

The ambassador got out of the car. They took me to police headquarters.

RÉPUBLIQUE DU TCHAD POLICE NATIONALE

The police officers wanted to ask me questions, but I told them I was too tired. So they threw me in jail.

It was a small, dirty room. There were mosquitoes, flies, and cockroaches. No food, no water.

BRING ME FOOD, BRING ME WATER!

They brought me a sheep's head and stinking eggs. I was alone. I was surprised.

At night, the guards would be drunk. They would make noise, kicking doors, fighting with each other.

JUST WAIT! THE PRESIDENT WILL SEE YOU SOON. HE'LL GIVE YOU A GOOD JOB!

In the morning, Reprieve's lawyers were allowed to visit me and asked why I was still being held. I was released after a week or so.

INITIALLY, THE PLAN WAS TO BRING YOU TO THE KEMPINSKI HOTEL...

CHRIS CHANG, investigator at Reprieve

The plan had been changed by the Minister of Interior and Security. Because many Goran Tribesmen were rebels, including members of my family, he was accusing me of being a rebel, and they had put me in jail.

```
(...)
Charge d'affaires spoke briefly June 19 with  Chadian Ambassador to the
U.S. Mahamoud Adam Bechir, who had  been part of the group of GoC
individuals to receive  al-Qarani from U.S. custody June 11, and who
remains in  N'Djamena handling the case.  Bechir stressed that although
the GoC wished to observe al-Qarani to determine how he would  handle
himself and who his associates would be, it did not  believe grounds
existed to keep him in custody or to bring  charges against him.
(...)
```

Cable from the U.S. Embassy in N'Djamena, dated 19 June 2009, leaked by WikiLeaks.

MOHAMMED?

After a few more days, some people came from the bush, from the Moussoro area, to see me. Among them were two of my mother's older brothers, Hamid and Mahamat, and more distant relatives of my father, along with their friends. They brought gifts — dates, jellabiyas, turbans...

THANK YOU!

COME LIVE WITH US! WE WILL GIVE YOU CAMELS. BE ONE OF US!

NO WAY! I COULD NEVER LIVE IN THE DESERT!

HA HA HA HA HA

Everyone in my family was in Moussoro, or Salal, and led a nomadic life, moving with the camels. People there are so poor, they have nothing.

Le Progrès (Chadian government daily), 23 June 2009

A life after despair:

Al-Gharani jubilates with his relatives

The Chadian ex-Guantánamo detainee meets his family

He looks 10 years older than his 21 years of age. Wisps of beard dot this young adult's face. But his sparkling eyes betray his youth, despite his height. The fatigue on his face reveals the fragility of his health. Mahamat Al-Gharani, the ex-young Chadian detainee, recently released from the American prison of Guantánamo (in Cuba), has just consulted a physician, on this Monday, 22 June 2009. The doctor prescribed him some antibiotic medicines. He has trouble adapting to the Chadian heat and the food of the capital, N'Djamena, which he is discovering for the first time in his life. Mahamat Al-Gharani, who was born and grew up in Saudi Arabia, is constantly getting visits from relatives, who welcome him. His close relatives keep him company in a dwelling placed at their disposal by a family member in the Diguel N'Gabo neighborhood, in the

Mahamat Al-Gharani (M.H.A.- PRG)

M. Al-Gharani with his relatives, in Diguel (M.H.A.- PRG)

eighth municipal district. 'When he first disappeared, we had completely lost hope to see him again alive one day,' says his maternal uncle, Mr. Mahamat Abdéramane. But the first sign of life from their son, who was arrested in Pakistan and transferred to Guantánamo, reached them around mid-June 2006 through some close relations residing in Europe. Four lawyers of different nationalities then gathered together to defend him. Mahamat Al-

Gharani was 14 when he was arrested by the Pakistani secret services, who appear to have 'sold' him to the CIA (the American espionage and counter-espionage service). The Central Intelligence Agency transferred him to Guantánamo, where he spent seven years in jail. As to the conditions of his arrest and detention, Mahamat Al-Gharani's relatives prefer to wait, before giving their opinion, for two of their son's lawyers, who will probably arrive this week.

To be continued p.4

I had forgotten the Goran language. I had forgotten almost everything. I had even forgotten some of my cousins in Saudi Arabia. They'd call me on the phone, and I wouldn't remember them!

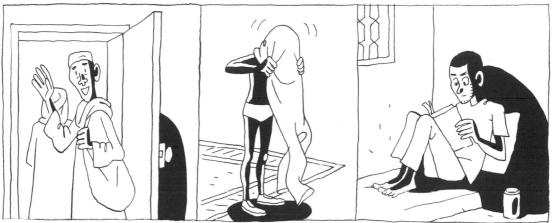

I stayed for five months in a house belonging to a small businessman of my tribe, in the Diguel Angabo neighborhood. There was no electricity, no water. I was alone there. People brought me food. Then the guy wanted to move in with his family, and I had to leave.

For six months, the International Committee of the Red Cross paid for a room for me, on rue des Quarante Mètres. Then, I shared a room with six roommates, all Gorans from Saudi Arabia.

I wasn't hanging out with anyone. I didn't understand the Chadians. They're different...

I tried to get work. I tried selling clothes in a shop belonging to a Goran trader, but I didn't know the Chadian currency, and I made mistakes. I decided to stop. Then I had an idea. I talked about it on the phone with a brother who had been released and was now living in Dubai.

AND WHAT ARE YOU DOING THERE IN, UH... AFRICA?

CHAD.

YEAH, CHAD, RIGHT. WHAT ARE YOU DOING THERE?

NOTHING.

FIND A JOB!

NO JOBS HERE. BUT I WANT TO OPEN A LAUNDRY... THERE'S NO LAUNDRY IN MY NEIGHBORHOOD. PEOPLE STILL WASH THEIR CLOTHES BY HAND!

GOOD IDEA!

THINK ABOUT IT, TELL ME WHAT YOU NEED, AND I'LL SEND IT TO YOU.

He sent me over, by plane, two washing machines and two tumble-dryers, at his own expense. They were stuck at the airport for six months, because I had no money to pay customs.

WHAT ARE THESE?

WASHING MACHINES.

DO THEY HAVE WHEELS? HOW WILL YOU MOVE THEM?

Meanwhile, I spent my days in front of my laptop.

Later in the afternoon, I'd play football with friends. I also tried to go jogging, but my back hurt. Torture had left its mark.

Since coming to Chad, the government had treated me badly.
The people of my tribe were happy to see me at first, and then
they grew scared. For all these reasons, I wanted to leave.

129

Soon after I arrived in N'Djamena, the Chadian security service phoned me.

SOMEONE TOLD US YOU CROSSED OVER TO KOUSSÉRI...

WHAT IS KOUSSÉRI?

JUST ANSWER THE QUESTION!

Kousséri is a Cameroonian town, just across from N'Djamena, on the other side of the river.

CHAD

N'DJAMENA

KOUSSÉRI

CAMEROON

I DIDN'T GO THERE.

IF YOU DIDN'T GO THERE, IT'S O.K.

AND IF I GO THERE, THAT'S ALSO O.K.!

TAKE IT EASY, WE'RE JUST LOOKING OUT FOR YOU.

The security service knew I wanted to leave Chad. But for that, I needed a passport, and the authorities refused to give me one.

In 2010, after five years of proxy war through their respective rebel groups, Chad and Sudan made peace. The border reopened and, even without a passport, it became easy to go to Sudan. I had friends in Khartoum, brothers who had been released from Guantánamo...

Sami al-Hajj:

THE BORDER IS OPEN, YOU SHOULD COME!

WALID MOHAMMED, Sudanese, former Guantánamo detainee, released in 2008.

THE SUDANESE AUTHORITIES ARE HELPING PEOPLE WHO WERE RELEASED FROM GUANTÁNAMO. THEY'RE GIVING THEM MONEY, JOBS, HOUSES...

WE WILL HELP YOU! COME, COME!

May 2010.

I took a small bag, the court papers that said I was innocent, and a few clothes. I gave the rest to friends and left. I thought I'd never go back to Chad.

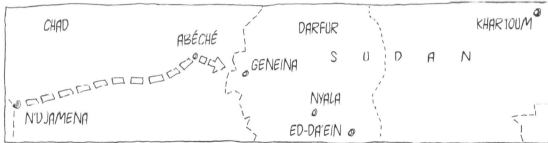

I took a bus to Abéché. Then I rode from Abéché to Geneina, in Sudan, in a pickup truck. Because of my back, I paid double to sit up front.

At the border, the Chadians don't ask you anything. They don't give a shit. The Sudanese ask you why you're coming here.

In Geneina, I found a room in a convoy of lorries going back to Khartoum after delivering food aid. It was a huge convoy; there were army cars escorting us, and sometimes helicopters overhead.

Between Geneina and Nyala, there were lots of checkpoints with armed men. Once, the convoy got spread out, and we were separated from the escort.

JANJAWID! SHUT UP, I KNOW THEM.

HASHISH...

HA HA!

SHUT UP!

SOME OF MY FRIENDS... THE JANJAWID TOOK THEIR MONEY AND KILLED THEM.

I'VE BEEN DRIVING FOR EIGHTEEN YEARS, I KNOW ALL THE ROADS.

I saw the war in Darfur and I felt sad. We passed burned villages, where no one lived anymore.

HERE, IT WAS A PARADISE BEFORE THE WAR... IT WAS VERY GREEN, A GOOD PLACE FOR A BREAK. BUT NOW IT'S NOT SAFE, WE'RE SCARED. WITHOUT AN ESCORT, WE WOULD BE KILLED...

GOVERNMENT OFFICIALS CAN'T ENTER THIS CAMP, OR THE PEOPLE LIVING HERE WOULD KILL THEM, BECAUSE THE GOVERNMENT KILLED THEIR FAMILIES. MANY PEOPLE SUFFERED, MANY PEOPLE DIED.

DARFUR IS A BEAUTIFUL PLACE, BUT AT THE SAME TIME, THE GOVERNMENT DIDN'T BUILD ANY GOOD ROADS, ANY HOSPITALS, NOTHING. NO MEDICINES, NO SERVICES. PEOPLE HERE ARE NOT ARABS, THE GOVERNMENT DOESN'T CARE ABOUT THEIR PROBLEMS...

We spent nine days in Nyala. The police were saying the road wasn't clear because of the rebels. Then one morning, we started moving east and reached Ed-Da'ein at night-fall.

We met another convoy, as big as ours, coming from the other direction. Those trucks from Khartoum were full of all kinds of goods; there were also fuel trucks. We slept together in Ed-Dae'in, and then both convoys moved out early in the morning.

Before we reached El-Obeid, people started calling us on their mobile phones.

THE OTHER CONVOY HAS BEEN ATTACKED. THE REBELS KILLED AROUND 70 PEOPLE.

THE ESCORT COULDN'T DO ANYTHING. MY FRIEND, WHO WAS IN THAT CONVOY, SAYS THE REBELS HIT IN THE MIDDLE, WHERE THERE WERE NO SOLDIERS. THEY TOOK SEVERAL TRUCKS.

KHARTOUM

EL-OBEID

NYALA

ED-DA'EIN

When we got to Khartoum, I called my brothers Walid and Adil.

WHERE ARE YOU NOW?

I DON'T KNOW.

I'M NOT FROM HERE. CAN YOU TELL MY FRIENDS WHERE WE ARE?

NO PROBLEM.

I felt good right away. I found the people in Khartoum very different from the people in N'Djamena. In Chad, if you lend your phone to somebody, he'll run away with it!

MY BROTHER!

ADIL HASSAN, former Guantánamo detainee, released in 2007

WELCOME TO KHARTOUM.

I was very tired, hungry, thirsty, and dizzy from the long trip — almost a month. I had been wearing the same clothes the whole time.

FIRST, EAT THIS.

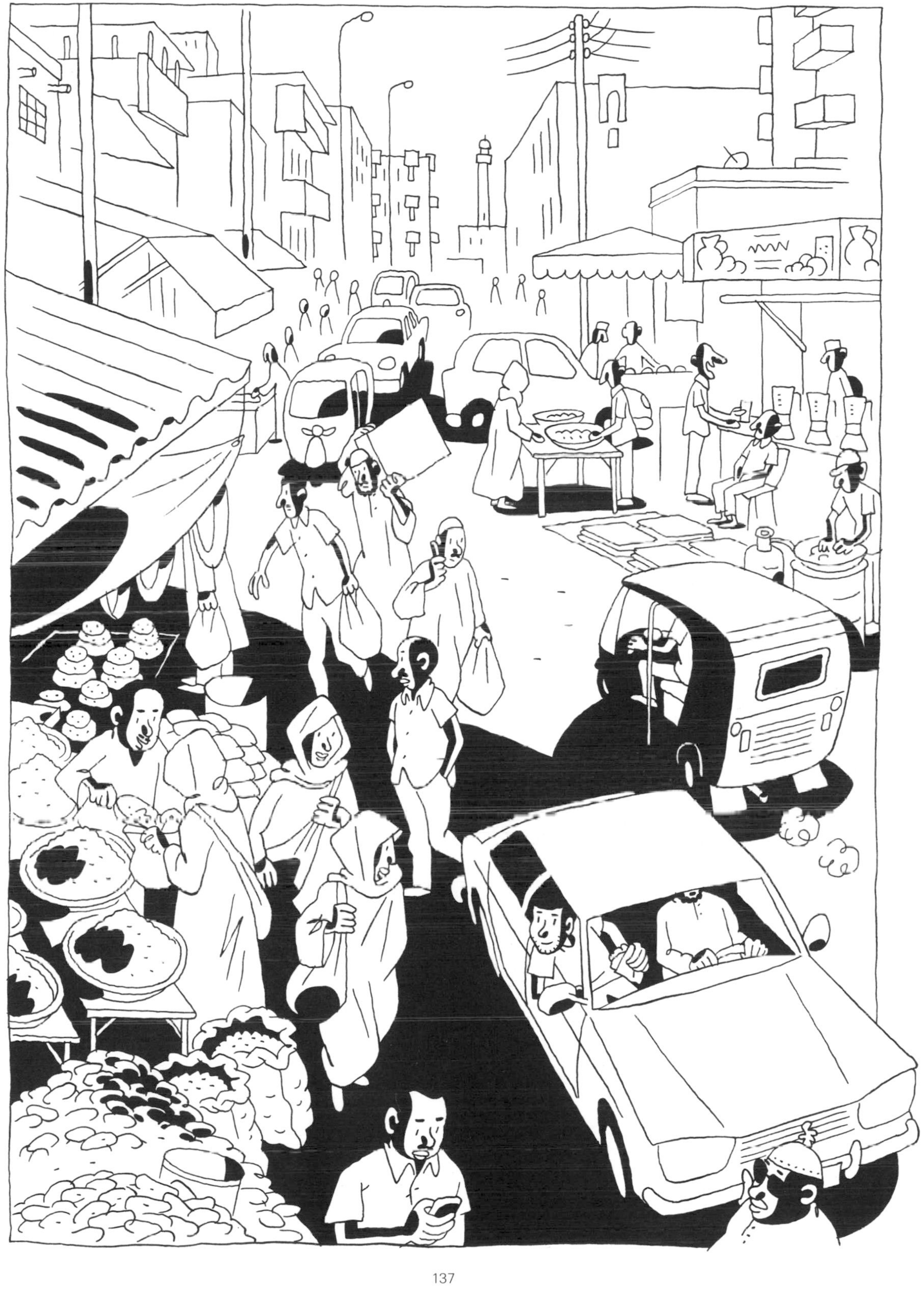

We arrived at Walid's.

SALAM ALEIKUM, MY BROTHER!

YOUR ROOM IS READY!

A good room, with A.C., a bed, magazines, books. I was very happy. I slept all morning and all afternoon. At 6 p.m., we went out to have dinner in a public garden.

WE HAVE A SURPRISE FOR YOU!

The surprise was Sami al-Hajj.

It was a surprise for him, too. He hadn't known I was in Khartoum.

HE'S STAYING WITH ME NOW!

OH NO, HE'S WITH ME! HE STAYS WITH ME!

O.K., THEN LET HIM SLEEP OVER JUST THIS ONE NIGHT, PLEASE.

I went to Sami's place. The next day in the morning, another ex-detainee invited us for breakfast.

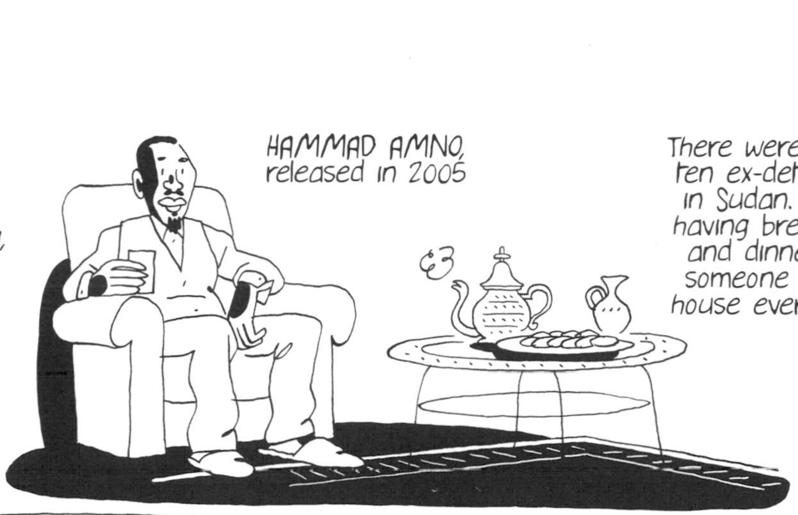
HAMMAD AMNO,
released in 2005

There were about ten ex-detainees in Sudan. I was having breakfast and dinner at someone else's house every day.

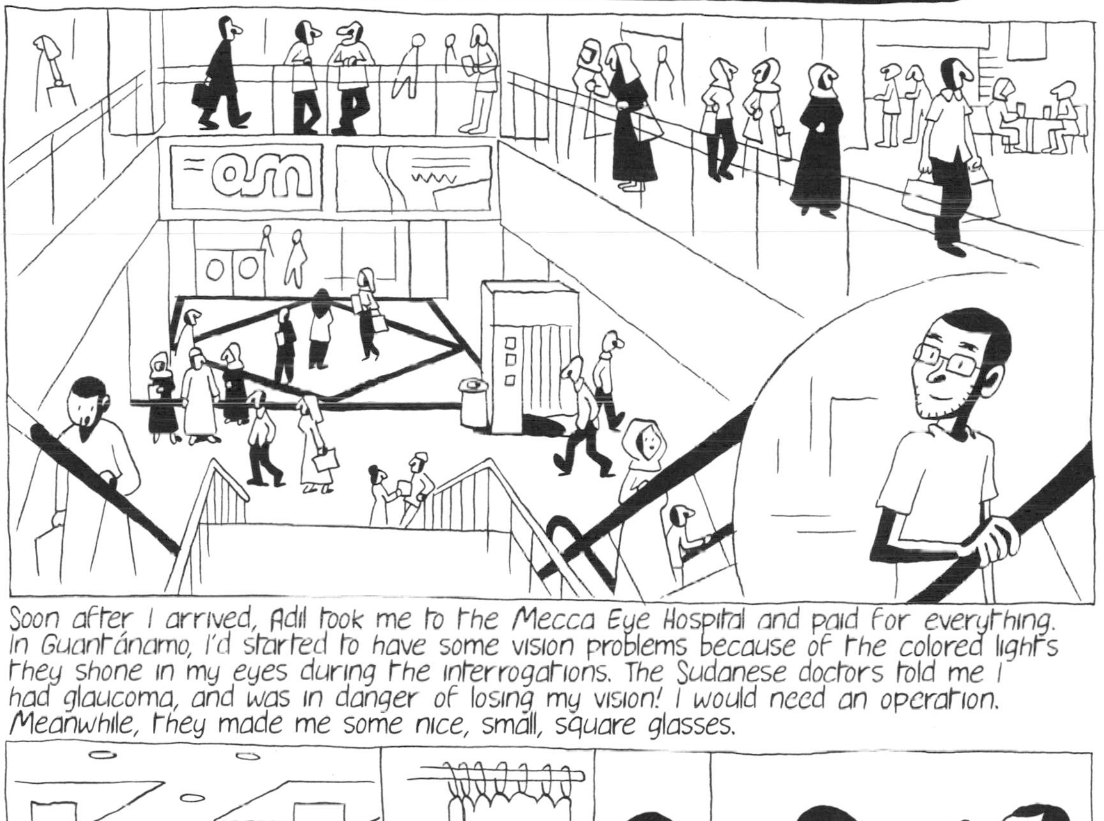
asn

Soon after I arrived, Adil took me to the Mecca Eye Hospital and paid for everything. In Guantánamo, I'd started to have some vision problems because of the colored lights they shone in my eyes during the interrogations. The Sudanese doctors told me I had glaucoma, and was in danger of losing my vision! I would need an operation. Meanwhile, they made me some nice, small, square glasses.

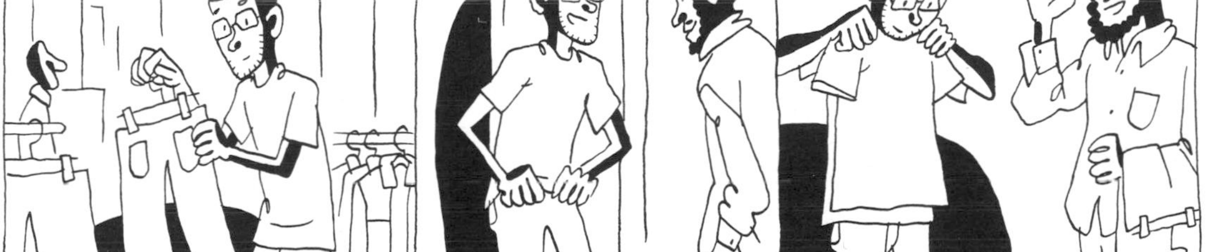

I made an appointment to see the doctor again. But then...

I had been in Khartoum for two weeks. It was a big city, at peace; I felt free, happy. One afternoon, after a meal with Sami, Walid, and other former detainees, I went shopping for jeans and T-shirts at a big mall with one of them, Abu Ahmad.

That day, someone kept calling my phone, but when I answered, no one was there. Abu Ahmad and I had gone our separate ways, so I called Walid.

They brought me to an old, dirty building, behind the official H.Q. of the intelligence and Security Services — you wouldn't guess it was even there.

WHY ARE YOU HERE IN SUDAN?

MEDICAL CARE. LOOK.

I showed them my stomach pills.

WHY DID YOU VISIT WALID AND SAMI?

THEY ARE MY FRIENDS.

O.K., O.K., WE KNOW ALL THAT, BUT WE WERE TOLD TO TAKE YOU TO JAIL.

MUSTAFA? THEY ARRESTED YOU TOO?

YES.

Mustafa was one of the ex-detainees with whom I had had lunch that day.

WHAT'S GOING ON?

I DON'T KNOW.

NO TALKING!

That same night, they moved me to Kober prison. I don't know what happened to Mustafa.*

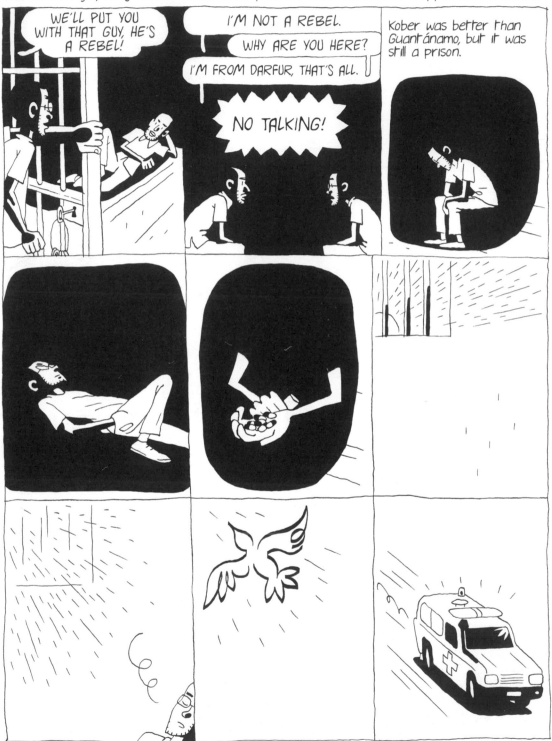

*Mustafa was not released for another two years.

I took all my stomach pills and passed out. They took me to the hospital. I spent all day there.

In the evening, I asked to go to the toilet.

I don't know how I did it, but I did.

In the street, the driver of the ambulance that had brought me to the hospital saw me, and started chasing me.

I kept running. I didn't know where I was going. I couldn't go back to Walid's. I just wanted to get as far away from Khartoum as I could. I ran all night.

I had no money, no phone. They'd taken everything from me in jail — my new glasses, my shoes. My feet were bare and started bleeding.

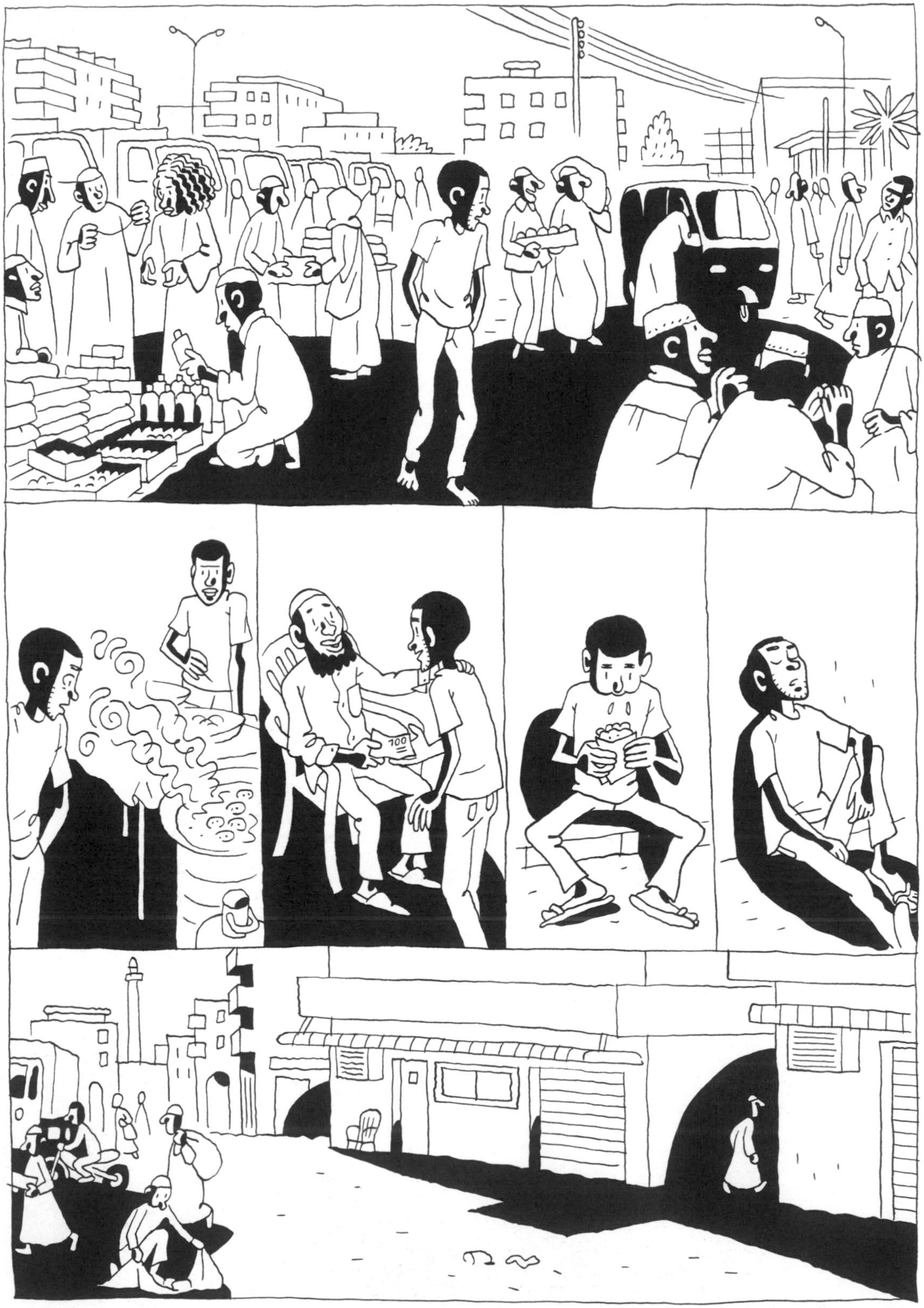
100

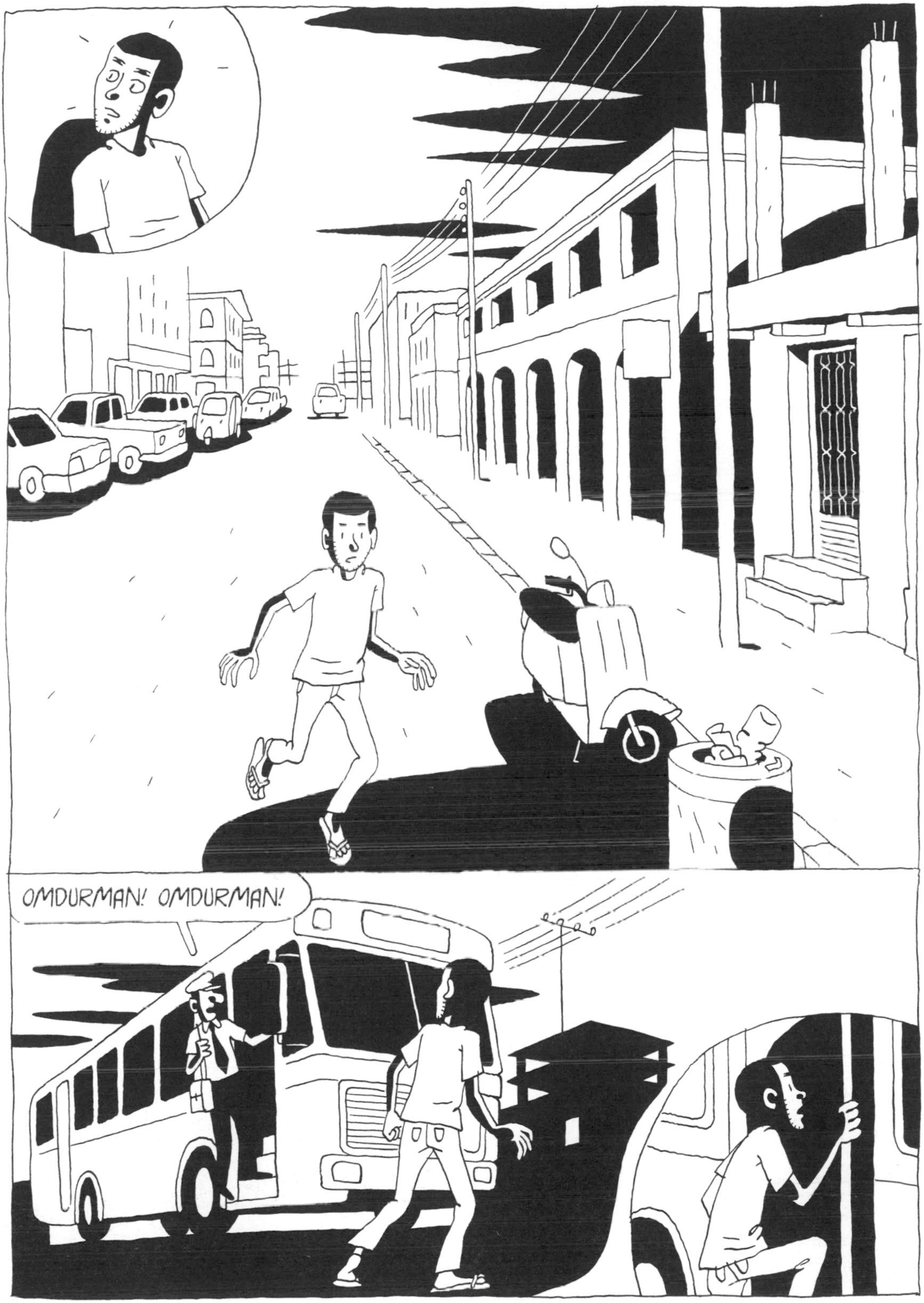
OMDURMAN! OMDURMAN!

I got to Omdurman. Then I went to Wadi Halfa, in the north. I spent two weeks there, then ten days in Dabbah.

There, I found some Goran and told them I had been robbed. I spent three nights in their house, then decided to go back to Chad. My trip to Sudan had been useless. I hadn't finished the treatment, and I had lost my glasses.

I recrossed the border in Tina. Since I was not allowed to go back to Medina, I would have to live in Chad.

I had left home to study, but had been prevented from doing so. I had been treated like a criminal, and they had taken eight years of my life.

I was thinking the same thing then as I had back in Guantánamo: I need to make my life better where I am. It is what it is.

(IS THERE) LIFE AFTER GUANTÁNAMO?

'Let me find a place to rest my head. / So tired. / It's not easy. / Life after Guantánamo. / Chad, Benin, Togo, Ghana, Niger, Nigeria. / All this, it's Americans who did this to me.'

That was the message my friend Mohammed El-Gharani sent me via Viber on 20 October 2017. We had met seven years earlier, shortly after his release from Guantánamo. We had kept in touch, in particular since the invention of WhatsApp and Viber. When Mohammed was doing well, his messages would become less frequent. When they came one after another, it meant he was calling for help. I was trying to alert the few organizations that could help him, ones that did not see Guantánamo as an indelible stigma. But I didn't know what more to do, from a distance.

All in all, we only met three times, most recently in June 2017. Each time, it was in the Chadian capital of N'Djamena, and always in a hotel room. I often asked to visit him at home, so I could meet the people he lived with, relatives or roommates. He always said no. Maybe he was ashamed to show me the poverty of his living conditions. Sometimes he'd waver, and we'd plan a home visit for the next day. But his relatives would persuade him to call it off. Not from shame: they were afraid that a visit would draw attention to them, and to him, the Guantánamo veteran.

•

N'Djamena, June 2017

A few years ago, N'Djamena only had two rather shabby *grands hôtels*: the Novotel and the Méridien. From their swimming pools, where French soldiers and Air France hostesses were taking a dip, one was afforded a view of the Chari river, marking Cameroon's border. The seasoned observer could see canoes loaded with sugar and other contraband goods crossing the river and, on the other side of the Novotel, on what was then one of the capital's only asphalt roads, military pickups chasing the smugglers immediately after they landed, sometimes knocking over an unfortunate pedestrian on the way.

Today, one can hardly see any of this. Blank concrete slabs have been erected between the Novotel and the river bank, intended to preserve rich guests, soldiers, and air hostesses from the invisible threat of the terrorist sect Boko Haram, operating in Cameroon, only a few hundred yards away. Unless they're there to screen out reality. The same feeling is even more present in the brand new Hilton hotel, a marble palace cut off from the poverty of the rest of N'Djamena. From my room, all I can see is an electric-green lawn, constantly being watered. Without that, the ground would probably be as dusty as the Chadian capital's invisible soil: and even as its sand laden air, whose harshness remains undiminished whenever I dare to open the window.

I've been invited to a conference on 'Preventing Violent Extremism'. Or in less politically correct words, Islamist terrorism: that of Boko Haram and other, more remote groups. From time to time, I leave the immense conference room where the experts are lecturing, to return to my bedroom and converse with Mohammed, who visits me every day. He knows a bit more about the topic than many specialists. All the accusations against him, beginning with that of having been member of a London al-Qaida cell in 1993, when he was barely six and had never left Saudi Arabia, proved unfounded. But before his innocence was finally acknowledged in 2009, he rubbed shoulders with some detainees with nefarious pasts. 'Some were afraid to talk about their pasts,' he told me shortly after his release. 'They feared you would repeat things to the interrogators and that they would be tortured.' However, he remembers an Afghan, whose name he prefers to conceal, who openly told other detainees that he was a member of both the Taliban and al-Qaida. His family had been killed by U.S. bombings. He was always telling the guards: 'You killed my family.' Then, after saying this, he would look sad. He would say: 'I didn't mean that guard personally killed my family. I just want him to think about it.'

The son and grandson of Chadian immigrants to Saudi Arabia, Mohammed was barely 14 when he was arrested in 2001 in Pakistan, where he had gone to learn English, hoping to get a job repairing computers. He was known as the youngest prisoner in Guantánamo. 'He was indeed the youngest detainee at the time of his arrest to be still in prison in 2004,' according to his lawyer Clive Stafford Smith, founder and director of the British charity Reprieve, which had mobilized for Mohammed. 'Three younger Afghans, between 10 and 13, had been detained in Camp Iguana and had just been sent back to Afghanistan. Younger prisoners had already been released when lawyers arrived in Guantánamo, but Mohammed was still there. The Americans really believed he was much older than he really was, that he was already adult when he was arrested.' When he was released, he was 21 or 22, and was sent back to Chad rather than to his country of origin.

I met him in N'Djamena the following year, in 2010. For two weeks, Mohammed told me about Guantánamo. Remembering 'Gitmo', as guards and prisoners call the prison, wasn't easy. Mohammed preferred to recall his friendships with some guards and 'brothers' (the co-detainees) and the moments of resistance, the brave deeds of the guerrilla war he had fought for eight years against the guards, thanks to violently desperate acts

– fighting, throwing piss and shit, and other exploits. His rebelliousness allowed him to cope, but it was also counter-productive, because in Guantánamo, any dissent, any insult towards the guards or the U.S. government, contributed to a justification for prolonged detention. But that did not prevent Mohammed from setting record levels of dissent. His eight years in Guantánamo were also his teenage years.

After a few days, we'd come to be less discreet. We had lunch in a restaurant and had even walked around town. A passer-by shouted at Mohammed:

'Hey, Gharani! How's it going?'

'You see', Mohammed whispered, half irritated, half proud. 'Here in N'Djamena, everyone knows Mohammed El-Gharani...'

He was wearing a hooded sweatshirt. I pointed out: 'Maybe if you wore a white djellaba like everyone else here, you wouldn't attract as much attention!' He told me his uncles who were living in the Chadian desert had offered him the same garment, as well as a turban.

'They asked me to come with them to the desert. They said they would give me camels. How can anyone live out there? I don't know how to put on the clothes they gave me! For eight years I've been wearing uniforms. Now, it's over, I'm free to pick my own clothes, I'm doing what I want.'

'And your beard? Don't you think that if you shaved, Chadians would be less suspicious of you being an Islamist?'

'I didn't have any hair on my chin when I was arrested, and it didn't prevent them from sending me to Guantánamo... My beard grew in jail, and now I keep it. I don't give a fuck!'

He apologized for the expression, one of those he learned from the guards in Guantánamo.

Mohammed is a strict Muslim. At the age of 6 he began attending Quranic school at the Prophet's Mosque in Medina, three hours a day. But he was also playing football every day, and so well that rival street teams were competing to have him as a player. At the time, he was a fan of Hamza Saleh, another Goran from Medina, who was playing with Jedda's al-Ahli club and had been selected twice for the national team, for the 1994 and 1998 World Cups. Even today, Mohammed supports Mohamed Noor, another black player, originally from Nigeria, who was selected for the Saudi team and obtained citizenship – the Holy Grail of which immigrant kids like Mohammed dreamt. He shows me racist commentaries on social networks in Arabic about the midfielder: slave, monkey, etc. In Guantánamo, Mohammed was one of the few black detainees, and also suffered from the guards' racism.

The more time I spent with Mohammed, the more it called into question my perception of what the world of a teenager who had grown up in Saudi Arabia was like. Able to faultlessly quote the Quran, Mohammed had been enjoying reading the novels of Agatha Christie, 'because her stories are so realistic'. Still further removed from real life, he loved playing on Wii, which he had discovered in Camp Iguana, where detainees stayed before their release. He played (virtual) boxing and table tennis against Uighur – the Chinese Muslim minority – co-detainees who were rather skilled ping-pong players. He listened to music, especially Bob Marley, to which his uncle Hamid had introduced him before he was jailed, but whom he had grown to like even more since his release, now that he spoke English and understood the lyrics.

Mohammed was a strict Muslim, but he had grown up among the youth of the Gulf who were feeling more and more constrained under the iron rule of aging, corrupt monarchs, and whose hopes were fed by a combination of Islamic values and the modernity conveyed by the Al Jazeera channel. That same youth

that, some months after our meeting, would be heading up the 'Arab Springs' that were about to appear across the region.

In N'Djamena's market, Mohammed couldn't understand why I'd bought an old carpet. 'In Saudi, we had the same carpets, but in synthetic fabric. Here it's camel hair! This is Chad!' As a child in Medina, he had enough of modernity, and that was what made him feel so uncomfortable in Chad: a country new to him, and which he found mostly archaic. 'I'm a foreigner here... What I see in N'Djamena, I tell my brothers and sisters and my cousins in Saudi, and they just don't believe me! How can you live here? I'd like to go to Europe.'

As we spoke, Mohammed would fall silent now and then, doubling up with pain. 'They hit me too much. Because of my stomach I have to hunch over like an old man. My back hurts too, and my knees, because we were forced to kneel so often.' At the time, one of his main reasons for trying to leave Chad was to receive medical care unavailable in N'Djamena. 'If I manage to leave, I'll get good treatment, I'll talk about Guantánamo in the media, and I'll go to court against the U.S. For justice, and to make sure people know. I don't believe the American people really understand. It's the American government that's responsible, not the American people.'

In late 2010, in between two meetings with Mohammed, I bumped into an American diplomat in N'Djamena's Novotel and managed to turn the conversation to the former detainee's case.

'All I know', the diplomat told me, 'is that there is an entirely classified agreement between the governments of the U.S. and Chad. This agreement asks Chad not to let El-Gharani out, and if ever he does get out, to inform us.'

'I know he needs to leave Chad to receive medical care that is not available here', I said. 'Why not let him get a passport and leave?'

'Because there's a risk. 25 per cent of the detainees released from Guantánamo have contacted or recontacted Islamist networks.'

According to the *New York Times* of 25 April 2011, 'By the Pentagon's count, as of Oct. 1, 2010, of the 598 detainees transferred from Guantánamo, 81 were "confirmed" and 69 "suspected" of engaging in terrorist or insurgent activities after their release. Accepting the highest Defense Department total, even the 25 per cent rate would be lower than most estimates of recidivism rates for federal and state ex-convicts.'

I asked the diplomat if the U.S. government was worried that Mohammed would take them to court. 'We don't care if he wants to sue the U.S. But... Good luck!'

'Are you saying "good luck" because he's talking about suing the U.S. government or because he was in Guantánamo?'

'Because he was in Guantánamo...'

•

It's June 2017, and I haven't seen Mohammed for seven years, but we immediately pick up again right where we left off. In my room at the Hilton, Mohammed sits on the armchair or settles on the bed, a pillow propping up his back – which still hurts. We talk for a long time, then break off, then start again. He takes a nap on the bed, showers, takes advantage of the hotel's internet to chat on WhatsApp with his family and friends abroad. He's a bit tired by the Ramadan fast that just began, but in much better shape than seven years ago.

Mohammed had once told me: 'Maybe one day I'll manage to leave Chad, but not tomorrow. It is what it is! I'll try to live my life, earn a living, get married.'

Shortly after our first meeting, in early 2011, Mohammed had married Amina, aged 18,

the daughter of a friend of his uncle, a Goran living in Saudi Arabia. His future father-in-law had been warned by a friend:

'Don't give him your daughter! He's dangerous, he could put a bomb somewhere!'

'Stop repeating that bullshit, or I'll tell my own daughter to go and blow you up! You don't even know this boy! I've known him since he was born. He's a good boy. Don't believe what you heard. He's innocent.'

Mohammed's parents flew to N'Djamena to attend the wedding. 'It had been almost ten years... But it was as if we had left each other the day before. I kissed the head and the hands of my mother, then of my father. We were all crying. They brought clothes, a phone, and the prescription glasses my uncle Musa had had made for me in Saudi. They were hoping I could come back to Medina with them. They stayed one month.' It was the last time Mohammed saw his father, who died in 2013.

Now a married man, Mohammed could no longer share a house with young bachelors, and rented another one for his wife and him. Now he also had to earn a living. His idea was to open a laundry. An ex-detainee 'brother' had sent him washing machines from Dubai, as a present, and he rented a small shop on the rue des Cinquante-Mètres 'I was doing fine at first, but in Chad, when you start to make money, policemen tend to visit you. In the morning, you go to open your shop, and you see a big padlock on the door and a notice telling you that you have to come to the police station.'

The police knew Mohammed had no papers, and was therefore not allowed to open a shop. He had to pay them $400 to $500 a week. 'The police took every profit I made. I was tired and decided to quit.'

By mid-2011, Mohammed and his wife managed to obtain passage in a car to Cameroon, then reached Benin, where

Amina's mother lived. In Cotonou, Mohammed underwent the stomach surgery he had not been able to get in Chad. And Amina gave birth to a daughter, Mariam. Their worries gradually evaporated. 'In Guantánamo, we all thought we wouldn't be able to have children, because they gave us so many injections I also got kicked down here ... [he indicates his groin] It still hurts when I piss.'

Mohammed didn't want to stay in Benin: he had learned English in Guantánamo and was hoping to settle in an Anglophone country. Ghana is no more than a few hours' drive from Cotonou. At the border, he had only to slip $100 into a policeman's hand.

The family settled in Accra. Mohammed continued his slow recovery – every two weeks, a doctor took care of his back, damaged at Guantánamo.

He struggled to find work, until he was hired by a Lebanese fruit-exporter – pineapples, mangoes, papayas, from Ghana to Beirut. Mohammed proved a quick study and decided to set up his own business. 'Friends in Medina found a supermarket, Mandarin, asking for one and a half tons of pineapples.'

More children followed. In 2014, a first son, whom Mohammed named Shaker, in homage to Shaker Aamer, his 'best friend in Guantánamo'. A year later, Shaker Aamer was released, after fourteen years in prison. And six months later, Mohammed had a second son, whom he named Musa, after an uncle.

Mohammed made friends. Fellow-foreigners and Ghanaians – in particular Ismail, a car dealer he met in the Batsonaa Mosque, where he often prayed, not far from his house. There were some he trusted enough not to hide his story. Those Moroccan construction workers in Ghana, say. They believed in Mohammed's innocence and introduced him to their cousin Lamiya, an educated young woman who worked for a big firm in Morocco. They got along well, and married in August 2016. Mohammed doesn't talk much about it, because he knows polygamy is not always well-viewed. But, as he often says, 'It is what it is!'. Mohammed was now renting two adjacent, back-to-back, houses, one for each of his wives. In Lamiya's house, he also put up his friend Ismail with his wife and children.

Business was going well, and Mohammed decided to invest all his savings in a bakery. He imported an oven and other appliances from Italy. In January 2017, the bakery-pastry-pizzeria 'Wow' opened on Spintex Road, the street where Mohammed was living.

I would have liked Mohammed's story to end here – happily. But his odyssey continued.

For there were also unpleasant encounters, from 'friends' who by no means wished Mohammed well. In 2013, he paid a visit to some Chadian students with whom he was on good terms. At their house, he met an old man named Saeed Hasan, a Muslim Ghanaian they had gotten to know in the mosque where they all prayed. He went by the title of 'Al-Hajji', given to those who had gone on the pilgrimage to Mecca, although he had not made it all the way there. 'If you need help, I know people in the government,' he told Mohammed. He introduced himself as a 'big man' a cousin of President John Mahama and of Baba Kamara, his security adviser.

'He knew I was from Gitmo, I guess he heard my story from the Chadian students,' Mohammed explains. 'I believe he told the intelligence services about me. Because some time afterward, an agent called me to say he wanted to meet me at a coffee shop. I was afraid, and immediately remembered Saeed Hasan and called him. We went together to the meeting. There were two plainclothes guys: King,* from the Intelligence Agency, and Bobby,* from Military Intelligence. Saeed told them he was one of them, that he was close to the President, and that I was his son, that he was my guarantor.'

Bobby and King asked Mohammed how he had made it to Ghana. 'The Americans are happy with the way you live here,' they said. Then they gave Saeed Hasan an envelope – 'for fuel' – and another one to Mohammed – 'Take this, for your travel expenses.' He opened it later and was surprised to see how much it contained: $300 – far more than what he'd had to spend on travel.

After the meeting, Saeed Hasan told Mohammed: 'They came to deport you to Chad; I'm the one who asked them not to do it. I'm your protector, it's only thanks to me you're safe.'

A few weeks later, he came back to Mohammed: 'I have to fetch and carry for you, so you can stay in Ghana for good. But I need some money to make things easier.'

The old man said he had to bribe important people to get them to sign documents. Since that day, Mohammed paid him regular sums of $200 to $400 each time Saeed pretended he had to pay a baksheesh to a 'big man'. All in all, Mohammed paid him $7,000.

He also continued his regular meetings with Bobby and King, always alongside Saeed Hasan. Each time, the agents gave Mohammed an envelope for 'transport', and another one to the old man, his guarantor.

Mohammed's relations with the intelligence services intensified in 2016. Ghana had agreed to welcome two other detainees released from Guantánamo, at U.S. request. Washington preferred to prevent them from returning to their country of origin, Yemen, which was at war, and where terrorist groups were active. In January 2016, Mahmoud Omar Mohammed Bin Atef, a.k.a. 'Faris', and Khalid Mohammed Salih al-Dhubi landed in Accra.

'What do you think of them?' Bobby and King asked.

'I didn't know them that well in Gitmo...'

Mohammed had met them in prison, but they were not his friends.

Unlike Mohammed's, their arrival was officially sanctioned and did not go unnoticed. The New Patriotic Party (N.P.P.), which was opposed to the government, and the opposition media all quickly understood they could exploit the affair and blame those in charge, accusing them of welcoming possible 'terrorists' and being a U.S. puppet. Shortly after the two Yemenis' arrival, as he was preparing a fruit shipment to Medina, Mohammed happened upon a discussion about them among airport staff, some pro-N.P.P., and others who supported the ruling National Democratic Congress (N.D.C.). One of them questioned Mohammed:

'See? the president brought two Gitmos to Ghana. What do you think?'

'Nothing! I'm here for the pineapples and mangoes, I'm not N.D.C., N.P.P. ... or even B.B.C.!'

The group laughed heartily at the joke.

'You don't talk politics, we know that!'

A few months later, when Bobby and King got back in touch with Mohammed, the tone had changed. This time, they were the ones who needed him. His job would be simple: calm down the two Yemenis, who were beginning to make trouble. 'They weren't happy,' Mohammed explained. 'The U.S. was paying Ghana money to care of these two, but the Ghanaians had put them up in bad apartments in a bad neighborhood and kept the money. The Yemenis had gone to the U.S. embassy to complain, and were threatening to talk to the media, and the Ghanaians didn't want problems with the U.S. ...'

Saeed Hasan took Mohammed to the Yemenis. They each lived in an apartment, one above the other. The walls weren't watertight, and when it rained, water leaked in.

'Look how they treat us! There's no tap water, no light for days. They should send us somewhere else! We'd rather be sent back to Gitmo! We want to go to the U.S. Embassy with a sign: "Take us back to Guantánamo!" We'll sleep in front of the U.S. Embassy. We've got nothing to lose!'

'Look,' Mohammed replied quietly. 'You can't act the same way you acted in prison. It's time to change!'

'Well, anyway you've changed! You don't talk like the guy we knew in Gitmo!'

'You're not in prison anymore, you can't solve problems by spitting on people's faces. In Gitmo, you had to do something before you got the right to talk, but not in the outside world. It's a different world. Ghana is a good country, but you need to be patient.'

Mohammed took note of the Yemenis' requests, and gave Saeed Hasan the list. Less than a week later, 'they moved them to a nice new estate, with a big swimming pool. Each had a house with five bedrooms. Their salaries had also increased, and each was given a car with a driver.'

Mohammed continued acting as a middleman between the Ghanaian authorities and the Yemenis. He translated their requests, showed them around Accra. He showed them where to buy clothes, took them swimming at their estate's pool or to the beach, played football with them. 'We became friends. I was just helping them to understand life. I was telling them they had to behave well, to be nice to the neighbors, or people would think all Gitmos behave badly.'

He visited them once or twice a week. Each time, he received $200 in an envelope. 'Now the envelopes made sense'.

Saeed Hasan also received envelopes. For the old man, the former detainee had become a godsend, and not only because the intelligence service was using Mohammed while keeping an eye on him. As early as 2014, Saeed Hasan had proposed to Mohammed that they do business together. In addition to fruit, Mohammed exported shea butter to the Gulf, highly prized by the cosmetics industry. Saeed explained he could supply him with raw material from his home region in northern Ghana. Mohammed gave him $30,000. No need for a receipt among friends. Two years later, Saeed had still not delivered the merchandise. He always had a good excuse. He was so busy he hadn't found the time to go back home and check, but the load was being packed, it was on its way.

In 2015, the United Nations office in Ghana owed $19,000 to a cousin of Mohammed who was selling cars in Benin. The transaction needed a Ghanaian bank account, and Saeed offered use of his. A year later, the cousin had still not received the money. He went with Mohammed to Kotobabi police station. Saeed immediately phoned Mohammed: 'I've been helping you out for so many years, and now you go to the police? If I get into trouble, you'll be in trouble too!'

Saeed promised to pay before the end of 2016. He was very busy, the election campaign was at its height, voting was going to take place in a few days, and he was hoping his cousin John Mahama would win again.

But on 7 December 2016, the opposition won the election. On 7 January, the new president, Nana Akufo-Addo, was sworn in. Saeed left Accra for his stronghold in the north of the country. Two days later, the intelligence service phoned Mohammed: 'You're El-Gharani? From Guantánamo? How did you get to Ghana?'

They summoned Mohammed and asked him not to meet with the two Yemenis anymore. 'All they knew about were two Gitmo people,' he said. The new regime was realizing that a third 'Gitmo' had slipped under the radar.

In March, an unknown number showed up on his phone screen: 'You're messing with Al-Haji Saeed? You don't know who you're playing with!' Mohammed thought the call had come from a street gang working for Saeed. He took precautions – his second wife moved to the first one's house. Only his friend Ismail and his family remained in the second house, in servants' quarters separated from the main building. One night, around 1 a.m., Ismail's number showed on Mohammed's phone: 'Six people with guns came looking for you. Thank God you weren't in the house!'

They had grabbed Ismail and punched him in the face.

'Where's El-Gharani?'

'He's not here! Look, the door is padlocked.'

They broke the windows to check inside. Soon after, a representative of the International Committee of the Red Cross went to Ghana to visit the two Yemenis. He phoned Mohammed and promised to discuss his case with the American authorities, advising him to get in touch with Navarro Moore, the Deputy Political Chief at the U.S. Embassy in Ghana. At the embassy gate, the guards refused to let Mohammed in. He finally ended up saying: 'I'm Mohammed El-Gharani, from Guantánamo'.

Immediately afterward, while Mohammed was still at the gate, his phone rang. 'Navarro Moore speaking. I know your story. I'll try to help you. But you shouldn't come here again. Attracting attention to the embassy is not good for us, or you either.'

The diplomat promised to mention Mohammed's case to someone called Ray,*

the intelligence agent in charge of the Yemenis since the change in government. Mohammed had just left the embassy when his phone rang again. It was Ray:

'Where are you?'

'In front of the U.S. Embassy.'

'You shouldn't go there. You're getting me in trouble with my boss. Let's meet right away.'

Mohammed met Ray in the Labone coffee shop, not far from the embassy. 'Look, Mohammed, only us guys at intelligence know you're from Gitmo. The new president, the ministers – they don't know. Don't go to the U.S. Embassy again. It will make things hard for us.'

In late March, I received a Viber message from Mohammed: he was afraid, he wanted to alert the Ghanaian media and asked me whether I would agree to speak in his favour at a local radio station. He was in touch with Captain Godsbrain Blessed Smart, the star presenter of Adom FM, the most popular station in Ghana. 'He's on every day between 7 and 10 a.m. Ninety per cent of the Ghanaians listen every day. And every day, he talks against corruption.'

Mohammed told his story to the presenter, who got enthusiastic: 'We have to put it on the air! The president has to hear this!'

Captain Smart immediately took Mohammed, in a vehicle painted with Adom FM colors, back to the U.S. Embassy. His idea was to put pressure on them: 'I'm Captain Smart from Adom FM, and I want to see Mr Moore,' he said at the gate. They were still at the gate when Ray phoned Mohammed, this time with irritation: 'What are you doing? Why are you going to the U.S. Embassy?'

It was not enough to discourage Captain Smart, who was determined to have a live broadcast with Mohammed. But the latter, more cautious, asked him to wait for a few days.

On 5 April, Mohammed was at the airport, waiting for a fruit shipment to Saudi Arabia to depart. Two officers from the Immigration Service came to him: 'Are you Mohammed El-Gharani?'

At that moment, Mohammed had a premonition: 'They're going to deport us to Chad, my family and me, and I'll be jailed again.'

After saying these words, some months after it happened, Mohammed stops talking, and a long silence falls over the hotel room in N'Djamena. Then he sighs: 'I've had enough.' He does not continue his story till the next day.

•

'They took me to their office downtown. They put me in a dark room with just a mattress. I had no clothes except shorts, and mosquitoes were biting me.'

After two days, Mohammed's wife Amina was authorized to visit him. He told her: 'Go and see Ismail, give him the eleven pages of the court order that proved me innocent, ask him to give Captain Smart the document, and tell him to go ahead with the broadcast.'

The same day, in the afternoon, an intelligence agent told Mohammed:

'We're sending you back to Chad.'

'Don't do this! Don't send me somewhere I don't belong!'

'You have no choice.'

First, he was driven home. Amina was there: 'They talked about you on radio today!' she exclaimed. Captain Smart, she told him, had even asked the National Security Minister how many former Guantánamo detainees were in Ghana. The minister had replied 'two', showing he did not know about or was trying to hide Mohammed's presence, which Captain Smart had now revealed.

The agents took Mohammed's two wives and his younger son Musa aboard a second car. The small convoy then headed for the Coastal International School, which the two other children attended. They had to leave their classrooms and got picked up too. The convoy then drove to the Bureau of National Investigations, surrounded by high concrete walls crowned with barbed wire. Mohammed was locked up alone in a cell, Amina and the three children in another, and Lamiya in a third one. The next day, Lamiya was sent back to Morocco.

On the evening of 9 April, Mohammed, Amina, and their children, escorted by three officers of the Immigration Service, flew to N'Djamena, where they were driven to the Department of Internal Security. In the building's yard, a plainclothes officer seated on a chair interrogated Mohammed, who had to remain standing. 'Did you do any terrorism like you did before? The U.S. don't keep someone in prison for eight years if they didn't do anything...'

'How can you live with people who believe you're guilty?' Mohammed asked me.

The guards kicked him and beat him with rifle-butts.

'Why?' he asked.

'There is no answer to that question,' was the reply.

Amina and the children were released in the morning. Mohammed was locked up in a room so dark he could hardly make out his hands. Gradually, he realized that other prisoners were there. More were thrown into the cell, maybe fifteen all in all. One had sold medication past its sell-by date; another had used a lost or stolen phone SIM card. 'We had no mattresses, we were sleeping on the ground. They beat us every day.'

After 25 days, Mohammed felt unwell. His blood pressure was too high. He was taken to the hospital. Since he was still a prisoner, three policemen were posted in front of his room. After a few hours, they were ordered to go back home. Mohammed was free. The next morning, an uncle came to pick him up.

Since then, he has lived in the house of a friend of his cousin Issa, who just this morning drove him to the hotel where we are talking. 'I'm sharing a room with five other men. My wife and kids are with her mum ten minutes' drive away. We left all our things in Ghana.'

When they arrived in Chad, all Mohammed and his family had were the clothes on their backs. The children landed wearing their school uniforms from Ghana. Since arriving here, they haven't been to school. Mariam tells Mohammed she wants to go back to her school, in Ghana. In N'Djamena, she doesn't play with the neighborhood kids. 'Look, Daddy, they don't even have real toilets here!'

Mohammed admires my hotel room's bathroom. When we're having a break, he enjoys taking a shower. One day, he runs a bath. 'I used to have baths in Ghana.' I interrupt him when I see water flowing under the bathroom door. In his euphoria, he'd let the bath overflow...

Before I leave Chad, I ask Mohammed what he would tell Barack Obama if he could talk to him. He replies: 'Shame on you. Don't promise something you can't do. You didn't close Guantánamo.'

Forty detainees remain in Guantánamo, 731 have been released, and nine died while in prison.

My plane takes off. I know that Mohammed will not stay in Chad for long. I know he can't keep still here. He promised his daughter Mariam: 'We're not going back to Ghana, but we won't stay in Chad either. We'll try to find a better place.' I worry. I fear that one day he might climb in the back of a pickup truck headed across the Sahara, and that he may end his days dying of thirst in the desert, drowning in the Mediterranean, or being held hostage or enslaved in Libya, like so many migrants.

On the morning of 13 September 2017, I receive this message: 'I left Chad. I have to run like a fugitive to save the life I live. I need your help before is too late.'

One week earlier, a relative, close to the Chadian regime, advised Mohammed to leave the country to escape a new arrest. He drove to Nigeria with two cousins. He went to Abuja, the capital, to get help from the United Nations High Commission for Refugees (UNHCR). On 9 October, he obtained a document recognizing him as an 'asylum seeker whose claim for refugee status is being examined'. Meanwhile – it can take months – this certificate is supposed to spare him from being sent back to Chad or any other country where 'his life or freedom' would be threatened.

In the meantime, Amina and her three children left Chad for another West African country, whose name it is better not to mention. In early November, Mohammed left Nigeria. After a twenty-hour drive and a $60 baksheesh, he joined his family. They had no housing and took refuge in a mosque. They spent the day in the yard, in the shade, except during prayer times, when the place was crowded. At night, like other homeless people, they slept on a large carpet in the next street along, which by then is quiet and cool.

Mohammed went back to Nigeria and managed to get back on his feet again. He opened a small restaurant – shawarma, rice, chips – hired a handful of Nigerian employees, brought his wife and kids over. Then – a new blow. One evening, he went back home to find his wife and kids had disappeared. 'I was worried all night, I couldn't sleep,' he told me the next day on the phone. In the morning, Amina called him from another country. She had left Nigeria suddenly, panic stricken after a big black car had pulled up in front of their house while Mohammed was away at the restaurant. Two men got out and told Amina they were from the Chadian Embassy. They asked about her husband, why he had come to Nigeria, how he'd gotten the money for the restaurant.

Mohammed's voice on the phone sounded scared. He decided not to sleep in his house again, then also left Nigeria to join his family in another West African country. By late 2018, he was still waiting for a 'safe country' to grant him asylum.

I have to stop here, although Mohammed's story is not yet done. I have a feeling that he will never give up the struggle, and will at last find a place where he will no longer be seen as a suspect, where he will be able to live a normal life – and finally be able to rest his head.

**Jérôme Tubiana,
December 2017–October 2018**

* Not their real names.

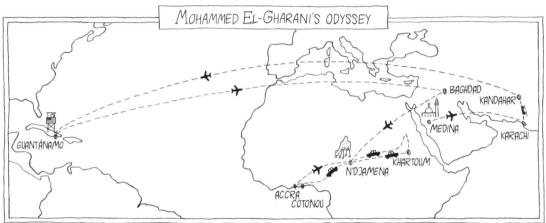

MOHAMMED EL-GHARANI'S ODYSSEY

MEDINA 1987-2001, KARACHI 2001, KANDAHAR 2001, GUANTÁNAMO 2001-2009, N'DJAMENA 2009-2011,
KHARTOUM 2010, COTONOU 2011, ACCRA 2011-2017, N'DJAMENA 2017

APPENDICES

Documents reproduced in this book

Several excerpts from official documents were repoduced on pages of this graphic novel. Some were leaked by WikiLeaks, while others have been made public. Of the latter, some have been redacted by the U.S. authorities.

Page 17. Excerpt from an FBI report on 'the FBI's Involvement in and Observations of Detainee Interrogations in Guantánamo Bay, Afghanistan and Iraq', 2008.
This document also gives a good example of redaction by the U.S. authorities:

V.   Allegations Regarding FBI Participation in Interrogation of Detainee Yousef Abkir Salih Al Qarani

In this Section we address the conduct of FBI agents, together with the military, in the interrogation of detainee Yousef Abkir Saleh Al Qarani (#269) at GTMO. We determined that in September 2003, FBI agents participated in a joint interview with the military that resulted in Al Qarani being short-chained and left alone for several hours, during which time he urinated on himself. In addition, at least one FBI agent participated in subjecting Al Qarani to a technique of disorientation and sleep disruption through frequent cell movement known at GTMO as the "frequent flyer program." We also examined additional allegations made by Al-Qarani during an OIG interview in March 2007 regarding FBI mistreatment.

A.   Background

FBI records indicate that Al Qarani's telephone number was found in the possession of other detainees known to be associated with al-Qaeda. At least 10 different FBI agents participated in interviewing Al-Qarani at GTMO between July 2002 and September 2003. The agents sometimes worked in pairs and sometimes conducted joint interviews with military investigators.

---

http://www.legal-tools.org/doc/81d5a3/pdf/

Page 43. Detainee Assessment of Yasin Basardah, 2008.

https://www.nytimes.com/interactive/projects/guantanamo/detainees/252-yasim-muhammed-basardah

Page 50. Excerpt from Camp Delta's Standard Operating Procedures (SOP), 2002, leaked by WikiLeaks.

https://wikileaks.org/static/pdf/US-DoD-DELTA-SOP-2002-11-11.pdf

Page 54. Detainee Assessment of Mohammed El-Gharani, dated May 2008.

This document also says: 'Detainee is an admitted member of al-Qaida and is assessed to be affiliated with the Global Jihad Support Network (GJSN) through his membership in a London, United Kingdom (UK)-based al-Qaida cell.'

This document was described by the *New York Times*, in a long article about it, as 'a case study in the ambiguities that surround many of the men who have passed through the prison at Guantánamo Bay'. According to the *New York Times*, Mohammed is described by the American military as 'the very incarnation of a terrorist threat'. The Assessment claims notably that Mohammed was arrested among al-Qaida fighters fleeing the battle of Tora Bora, in Afghanistan. Seven years after his arrest, this document still rates him as 'high risk' and recommends him for 'Continued Detention'.

https://www.nytimes.com/interactive/projects/guantanamo/detainees/269-mohammed-el-gharani

Page 71. The description of the organization of the Immediate Reaction Force (IRF)'s Team is excerpted from Camp Delta's (revised and updated) Standard Operating Procedures (SOP), 2003.

http://www.comw.org/warreport/fulltext/gitmo-sop.pdf

Page 83. The 'Muslim burial' sketch is taken from the same document.

http://www.comw.org/warreport/fulltext/gitmo-sop.pdf

Pages 104-105. Excerpts from Judge Leon's Decision.

https://ecf.dcd.uscourts.gov/cgi-bin/show_public_doc?2005cv0429-202

Page 117. Excerpts from a cable from the U.S. Embassy in N'Djamena, dated 9 November 2007, leaked by WikiLeaks.

http://wikileaks.wikimee.org/cable/2007/11/07NDJAMENA876.html

Page 125. Excerpt from a cable from the U.S. Embassy in N'Djamena, dated 19 June 2009, leaked by WikiLeaks.

http://wikileaks.wikimee.org/cable/2009/06/09NDJAMENA244.html

Bibliography

Mohammed El-Gharani's story was first published in the French magazine *XXI* and in the *London Review of Books*:

Jérôme Tubiana, "Le gamin de Guantánamo" [The Kid from Guantánamo], *XXI*, No. 15, July–September 2011.
Mohammed el Gorani and Jérôme Tubiana, "Diary", *London Review of Books*, 15 December 2011.
A shorter version of the afterword was also published in France as "Guantánamo: la vie d'après" [Life after Guantánamo], *Le Nouveau Magazine littéraire*, March 2018.

Other sources

Laurie Anderson, "Bringing Guantánamo to Park Avenue", *New Yorker*, 23 September 2015.

Mourad Benchellali, with Antoine Audouard, *Le piège de l'aventure* [The Adventure Trap], Robert Laffont, 2016.

Lakhdar Boumediene and Mustafa Ait Idir, *Witnesses of the Unseen: Seven Years in Guantanamo*, Redwood Press, 2017.

Annick Cojean, "Mohammed, adolescent, innocent et détenu à Guantánamo" [Mohammed: Teenaged, Innocent, and Detained at Guantánamo], *Le Monde*, 19 November 2005.

Marc Falkoff (ed.), *Poems from Guantánamo*, University of Iowa Press, 2007

William Glaberston and Charlie Savage, "Secret Case Against Detainee Crumbles", *New York Times*, 26 April 2011.

Scott Horton, "The Guantánamo 'Suicides'", *Harper's Magazine*, March 2010.

Andrea Jones, "Growing Up Guantánamo", *ViceNews*, 11 November 2014.

Mohamedou Ould Slahi, *Guantánamo Diary*, Little, Brown and Co., 2015.

Frank Smith, *Guantanamo*, Les Figues Press, 2014.

Clive Stafford Smith, *Eight O'Clock Ferry to the Windward Side*, Nation Books, 2007.

Michael Winterbottom (dir.), *The Road to Guantánamo*, 2006.

Andy Worthington, *The Guantánamo Files*, Pluto Press, 2007.

Acknowledgements

To Alex Kotlowitz and Paul Salopek, who led me to Mohammed; Clive Stafford Smith, Chris Chang, Polly Rossdale, Katie Taylor, and everyone at Reprieve who supported this project; Patrick de Saint-Exupéry (*XXI*), Joanna Biggs and Jeremy Harding (*London Review of Books*), and later Raphaël Glucksmann and Hervé Aubron (*Le Nouveau Magazine littéraire*) for their immediate enthusiasm for Mohammed's story; Pauline David (Amnesty International) for the idea to turn it into a graphic novel; Vincent Henry and André Kadi 'Soulman' for their efforts; Sophie Furlaud for her crucial encouragement; Jonathan Littell for his many kindnesses; Yves Prigent (Amnesty International), Mourad Benchellali and Sarah Tick for their advice and help spreading the word; my French publisher Pauline Mermet for bringing this seemingly endless project to a conclusion, as well as Sophie Castille and everyone at Dargaud who believed it could cross borders; and last but not least, Emma Hayley and everyone at SelfMadeHero: what better name could there be for the story of someone like Mohammed?

J.T.

Guantánamo and Amnesty International

Amnesty International is the world's largest human rights organization. Together with eight million supporters worldwide, we stand up for human rights, believing that everyone has the power to change the world for the better. We seek to protect people wherever justice, fairness, freedom, and truth are denied. Human rights belong to all of us, no matter who we are or where we live.

Since its opening in 2002, roughly 780 prisoners of war have been controversially detained at Guantánamo Bay. At the time of writing, 40 still remain there. Mohammed El-Gharani's story is unfortunately all too familiar. The facilities at Guantánamo have become a symbol of the gross human rights abuses perpetrated by the U.S. government in its 'war on terror'.

> 'Over the years, Guantánamo has come to symbolize torture, rendition, and indefinite detention without charge or trial – in complete violation of internationally agreed standards of justice and human rights. Its closure is both essential and long overdue.'
>
> **— Erika Guevara-Rosas,**
> Americas Director, Amnesty International

With the Trump administration signing an executive order to keep the prison open indefinitely in 2018, it is more important than ever to read stories like *Guantánamo Kid*. Since Amnesty was founded in 1961, individuals all over the world have sent millions of letters, emails, and faxes as acts of solidarity and protest. Shaker Aamer, a Guantánamo detainee released in September 2018 after 13 years in detention, is just one of the recipients. This simple action gives people hope and inspiration, letting them know that they have not been forgotten. It also sends a message to the authorities that people around the world are watching what they do.

You can take action on behalf of individuals whose human rights are being violated. Your support really can change someone's life, and your solidarity can help make the world a better place.
For more information, visit:

www.amnesty.org.uk/actions
www.amnestyusa.org/take-action

And please also remember that situations change – so do check our website for up-to-date information before you take action.